A SUCCESSFUL LIFE IS
A RACE OF FAITH

"Cynics call life a rat race; I call it an exciting marathon with new challenges around every bend," says Robert A. Schuller. "So let's put on our track shoes and go for the Gold! Let's take the faith and run the race, believing it is God who offers everything worth having in life. Never stop believing. Never quit on God, because he never quits on you."

The prize is true freedom. Are you ready to enter the race?

POWER TO GROW
BEYOND YOURSELF

ROBERT A. SCHULLER, son of the world-renowned preacher Robert H. Schuller, is the pastor of the Rancho Capistrano Community Church in San Juan Capistrano, California. He is the bestselling author of *Getting Through the Going-Through Stage*, and the editor of *Robert Schuller's Life Changers* and *Robert H. Schuller Tells You How to Be an Extraordinary Person in an Ordinary World*.

By Robert A. Schuller
from Jove

ROBERT SCHULLER'S LIFE CHANGERS
Edited by Robert A. Schuller

ROBERT H. SCHULLER TELLS YOU HOW TO BE
AN EXTRAORDINARY PERSON IN AN ORDINARY WORLD
Edited by Robert A. Schuller

POWER TO GROW BEYOND YOURSELF

ROBERT A. SCHULLER

POWER TO GROW BEYOND YOURSELF

JOVE BOOKS, NEW YORK

POWER TO GROW BEYOND YOURSELF

A Jove Book / published by arrangement with
Fleming H. Revell Company

PRINTING HISTORY
Fleming H. Revell edition published 1987
Jove edition / August 1988

ISBN: 0-515-09677-6

Jove Books are published by The Berkley Publishing Group,
200 Madison Avenue, New York, New York 10016.
The name "JOVE" and the "J" logo
are trademarks belonging to Jove Publications, Inc.

PRINTED IN THE UNITED STATES OF AMERICA

10 9 8 7 6 5 4 3 2 1

ACKNOWLEDGMENTS

Unless otherwise identified, Scripture quotations are author's paraphrase.

Scripture quotations identified NASB are from the New American Standard Bible, © The Lockman Foundation 1960, 1962, 1963, 1968, 1971, 1972, 1973, 1975, 1977.

Scripture quotations identified NIV are taken from the HOLY BIBLE: NEW INTERNATIONAL VERSION, copyright © 1973, 1978 by the International Bible Society. Used by permission of Zondervan Bible Publishers.

Scripture quotations identified PHILLIPS are from THE NEW TESTAMENT IN MODERN ENGLISH, Revised Edition—J. B. Phillips, translator. © J. B. Phillips 1958, 1960, 1972. Used by permission of Macmillan Publishing Co., Inc.

Verses marked TLB are taken from *The Living Bible,* copyright © 1971 by Tyndale House Publishers, Wheaton, Illinois. Used by permission.

Material from THE DOUBLE WIN by Denis Waitley, copyright © 1985 by Denis E. Waitley, Inc. Published by Fleming H. Revell Company. Used by permission.

Material from ROBERT H. SCHULLER TELLS YOU HOW TO BE AN EXTRAORDINARY PERSON IN AN ORDINARY WORLD, edited by Robert A. Schuller, copyright © 1985 by Robert A. Schuller. Published by Fleming H. Revell Company.

Material from ROBERT SCHULLER'S LIFE CHANGERS, edited by Robert A. Schuller, copyright © 1981 by Robert A. Schuller. Published by Fleming H. Revell Company.

Contents

INTRODUCTION

This book was conceived during a visit to the home of the great film actor Gregory Peck, who invited my father and me to a preview of his latest project. It was a time in my life when I needed a lift, but I never dreamed how helpful it would be to interact with this talented and caring man.

After greeting us warmly, Mr. Peck explained that for the last eighteen months, he had been working on something which had consumed his entire being, something he "had always wanted to do." He had tape-recorded the entire Bible, an experience he called one of the greatest and most fulfilling challenges of his life. And now he wanted to play some of his recording for us.

After spending a few moments over a cup of coffee in his living room, we all walked down a narrow path that wound through his five-acre estate to a small log cabin nestled among massive trees. He introduced us to his son, who had been the technical engineer of the taping, done in the tiny log cabin. Here Mr. Peck had spent countless

hours reading and rereading to perfection every word of
the Old and New Testaments.

"I've selected a passage that I hope you will find appro-
priate," he told us. "It's the eleventh chapter of Hebrews.
I think you'll be interested in hearing this."

Suddenly I heard, in the resonant recorded tones of this
exquisite actor, "Faith is the assurance of things hoped
for, the evidence of things not seen. . . ."

I was entranced and remained so as I listened to his
reading of the entire text of Hebrews 11, which contains a
veritable "Hall of Fame of Faith" that includes some of
the most courageous personalities in the Bible.

I was so inspired and uplifted by Gregory Peck's reading of this dynamic passage of Scripture that I couldn't
wait to get back to my study to start developing a new
series of messages on how to live by faith. I preached that
series to my congregation at Rancho Capistrano Community Church in San Juan Capistrano, and many of our
members were moved and inspired toward living a life of
faith that they had never understood before.

From that series came this book, in which my purpose is
to help you rethink your faith and come to a new apprecia-
tion of how God can work in your life. I believe the
business of living is summed up in this familiar motto:

> *Work as if it all depends on you*
> *Pray as if it all depends on God.*

That may sound a bit simplistic to some, but it has been
a very freeing thought for me. For many years I struggled
with the challenge of how to know God's will for my life.
I was told to read the Bible and pray and I would receive
direction. I spent countless hours studying and praying in
the hope that I would learn exactly what God wanted me to
do.

I got a great deal of general direction from Scripture,
but the answers to specific questions were elusive. It was
easy enough to know what *I* wanted to do in certain

situations, but that wasn't what mattered most to me. *I wanted to do what God wanted,* and in many cases it was hard to know what His will might be.

Then one day two sentences from the New Testament seemed to leap off the page with new meaning. The Apostle Paul, one of the most cogent thinkers the world has ever known, writes:

> ". . . be keener than ever to work out the salvation that God has given you with a proper sense of awe and responsibility. For it is God who is at work within you, giving you the will and the power to achieve His purpose."[1]

These words make up verses 12 and 13 of the second chapter of Paul's letter to the Philippians. Here he strikes a clear balance between working as if everything depends on you and praying as if everything depends on God.

When Paul uses the word *salvation,* it may bring to mind pictures of heaven and eternity, but I believe he is also thinking about what happens on earth. When Paul talks about salvation—being saved—he also speaks of the power that overcomes our present weaknesses and failures, and enables us to succeed in life.

In verse 12 he advises us to work out our salvation, a gift from God, by always keeping a proper attitude of respect for Him and a sense of our own responsibility. I had been trying to do just that, but I had still struggled with knowing what God wanted me to do in certain situations.

In verse 13, however, Paul gives the answer: While I am working out my salvation, *God is at work within me* giving me the will, power, and courage to achieve what He wants! Paul is describing salvation as something for the here and now as well as eternity later. Paul doesn't say God has done His work, or that He will do it later. He says *God is working in my life right now* to change it for the better!

At last I saw it. I was free from wanting my will instead of God's will, but I was also free from feeling I had to be a puppet whose will is enslaved to God. For the first time realized that my will *was* God's will, *as long as I followed His teachings in Scripture*.

God Is Not Our Puppet Master

Since I made this discovery, my readings in psychology have verified that following Paul's advice is a very healthy way to live. No one is forcing you to do things you don't really want to do, but at the same time you become responsible for your actions. You can't blame your friends, your employer, your spouse, or your children.

Above all, you can't blame God and see Him as some kind of puppet master who is dangling you by strings. If you have freely accepted His love and salvation and want only what He wants for your life, you are not a puppet. You are free to live according to God's instructions, which He has provided in the Bible.

On a trip to the Holy Land, I experienced a striking illustration of how I am not enslaved to God's laws, but am free to use God's laws as a means of direction, encouragement, and security.

Our party had checked into a newly constructed hotel in Jerusalem, which had opened for business even though some finishing touches needed to be done. I went up to my room on the fourteenth floor and unpacked. I walked over to a sliding glass door that led to a balcony outside, and attempted to go out to enjoy the spectacular view from fourteen floors up.

To my surprise, I found a wooden dowel inserted in the sliding-door track, which prevented the door from being opened. I looked out on the balcony and saw why. There were no railings! Obviously this was one of the finishing touches to be done by the construction crew.

But it's a lovely view, I told myself. *I'll be careful.*

removed the dowel and slid the door open. I took one step onto the balcony and suddenly realized that I really wasn't that interested in the view after all! Without the railing, I felt very high up and very unsupported. I quickly stepped back into the room, shut the door, and put the dowel where it belonged. I did not venture out on that balcony again while staying in the hotel.

A day or two later we moved on and checked into another hotel. Again my room was near the top floor, and once again it had a balcony. This time, however, there was also a railing on the balcony. I walked out on the balcony, leaned over the rail, and gazed down to savor the magnificent view of the city. Then I turned around, leaned back on the railing, and enjoyed the late-afternoon breeze. Next, I walked up and down the balcony, fully enjoying every foot of its pleasures and every inch of the panoramic view it afforded.

God's laws are like a railing around a balcony. Without the railing, we cannot enjoy the outer limits of life and grow beyond ourselves.

Paul goes on to say that besides direction and security, God gives you *"the power* to achieve"! Because you seek to glorify Him and achieve His purposes, you can do what you want to do, be what you want to be, and achieve what you want to achieve!

People say, "I *have* to go to work!" That's not really true. You live in America and you have the freedom *not* to go to work. But with that freedom comes responsibility. What would you do if you didn't go to work? Would you sit at home and watch soap operas? Is what you gain by going to work more rewarding and self-gratifying than staying home? If so, then take the responsibility for your actions and say, "I *want* to go to work," instead of giving your freedom away and removing yourself from your responsibilities by saying, "I *have* to go to work!"

For several years now I have been doing what I want to do, working as if everything depends on me, and praying as if everything depends on God. Wanting what God wants assures me that His will is my will. My life runs much more smoothly because I know God is at work in me achieving His purpose.

Who Is in Charge, Man or God?

I like to think that my work/pray philosophy is a sensible solution to the running battle theologians have fought over the centuries as they argue the differences between human free will and divine sovereignty. Is one more important than the other, or can they overlap?

At one pole are those with what is often labeled a "liberal" view that stresses man's free will. They say God created the world a few billion years ago, put it in motion, and now He's watching us do what we can to make it all work. Man is in charge, more or less.

At the other pole are those with an ultraconservative view that claims human will and freedom are practically nonexistent. We are all predestined to act the way God wants us to act. While the ultraconservatives don't like the analogy, this view reduces us to puppets. We may think we are acting freely, but God is really pulling our strings.

Between these two extremes lie all kinds of viewpoints that seek a middle ground. I believe we are to take responsibility to work out our salvation in this life, knowing that God is at work within us to help us succeed and achieve His purpose by praying as if it all depends on God and working as if it all depends on us.

Tune in Your Mind to God's Mind

Is it possible to always work as if everything depends on you and pray as if everything depends on God? I believe it is, if we tune in our minds to God's mind. How do we do that? Through prayer. As Paul says, "Pray without ceasing."[2] When you believe God and put your faith in Him daily, you join your thought processes to His. You find that "praying without ceasing" is possible. And you know God will work out His purposes in your life. Believe it! Not because you have to, but because it works!

In the chapters that follow, we'll see why and how faith is the motivating force that helps you:

. . . develop the right attitudes.
. . . conquer your fears.
. . . seek excellence instead of mediocrity.
. . . dare to leave the ruts and become all you were
      meant to be.
. . . never stop learning.
. . . set goals and achieve them.
. . . hope against hope, even when life looks its darkest.
. . . give of yourself as you give up self-centeredness.
. . . go for a perfect 10 with God.

I've learned all these lessons the hard way, and I want to share them with you. Cynics call life a rat race; I call it an exciting marathon with new challenges around every bend.

So let's put on our track shoes and go for the Gold! Let's take the faith and run the race, believing it is God who offers everything worth having in life. Never stop believing. Never quit on God, because He never quits on you. As the poet said:

> *Success is failure turned inside out—*
> *the silver tint of the clouds of doubt—*
> *And you can never tell how close you are,*
> *It may be near when it seems afar;*
> *So stick to the fight when you are hardest hit—*
> *It's when things get worse that you mustn't quit!*[3]

1

Your Attitude Will Make the Difference

RECENTLY, MY SIX-YEAR-OLD nephew Jason was moping around the house getting in his mother's way. She suggested he run out in the backyard and play. Jason argued a bit, but finally went outside, threw himself on a chaise lounge, and wailed, "Oh, I *always* have to play. It's so *hard* to play! It's such hard *work!*"

Remember the cliché "One man's work is another man's play"? One little boy's "work" is what would be play to many of us. We see the same principle in effect everywhere. What might be work for you could be play for your spouse, your neighbor, or your friend, and vice versa. It depends on your attitude.

Attitude has always been important in the Schuller family. My four sisters and I grew up repeating the lines of Ella Wheeler Wilcox every day before we left for school:

> *I'm going to be happy today,*
> *Though the skies may be cloudy or grey,*
> *No matter what comes my way,*
> *I'm going to be happy today.*

My father is the one who taught us that the brain is like a radio. One of his favorite lines each morning was, "You have to learn to turn your dial." Whenever I came to the breakfast table with a sad or grumpy face, Dad would stop and say, "Wait, wait a minute, wait, wait, wait. Stop everything. Robert, turn your dial."

As a child, I didn't always appreciate Dad's advice to "turn my dial," but now, as a parent myself, I find I am using this same advice with my own children. The human will is like a radio. You can tune it to the station you wish. You don't have to wear a sad face. You don't have to be unhappy. You can turn your dial to a happy face and you can think pleasant thoughts, not grim and foreboding ones. Your attitude can be whatever you want it to be. Just turn your dial!

Admittedly, it isn't always easy to turn your dial. Sometimes it takes discipline. Often it takes courage. Above all, it takes faith—believing that there are always possibilities in life that make turning your dial worthwhile.

I am sometimes asked, "Do you really believe in possibility thinking?" My answer is an unhesitating, "Yes!" I believe in possibility thinking because it has worked for me when I needed to take an idea and carry it to completion. I know possibility thinking works because I have seen faith work time and again in my own life and ministry.

As I shared in the Introduction, the inspiration for this book came from listening to the deep baritone voice of Gregory Peck as he read the eleventh chapter of Hebrews from the New Testament. That chapter opens with words that are tailor made for every possibility thinker who ever lived.

> Now faith is the assurance of things hoped for,
> the conviction of things not seen.[1]

Hebrews 11 has been called the "Hall of Fame of Faith" because it lists "saints of old" who won a reputation for their great faith.[2] They also gained fulfillment, peace of mind, joy, love—in short, success in life. Hebrews 11 is a literal "who's who" of possibility thinkers who succeeded because they trusted in God's power to grow beyond themselves.

A Study in Attitudes

I will be forever thankful to my father and mother for rearing my four sisters and me to have faith and think positively about life no matter what happens. I sometimes wonder how much difference possibility thinking might have made in Adam's family. He and Eve had two boys, Cain and Abel. The Book of Hebrews tells us, "It was by faith that Abel obeyed God and brought an offering that pleased God more than Cain's offering did. God accepted Abel and proved it by accepting his gifts; and though Abel is long dead, we can still learn lessons from him about trusting God."[3]

The story tells us that both sons offered sacrifices to God, but God accepted Abel's gift while refusing Cain's. Why would God accept one gift but not the other? We can't be entirely sure, but it had something to do with attitudes.

Abel was a keeper of flocks and brought to God a "firstling"—the best animal he had. Cain was a tiller of the soil and he brought an offering to the Lord of the fruit of the ground. God refused the fruit. Was something wrong with the gift? Was it the best Cain could grow? To get the whole story we have to go back to Genesis 4. God doesn't describe Cain's gift but He does tell him he hasn't done well to give what he did and that sin could be "crouching at the door."[4]

You would think that getting confronted that way by God Himself might impress Cain enough to listen up and change his attitude. God even told him that though sin desired him, he could master it. But not so. Sometime later Cain waited for his chance and then murdered his brother while they were alone in a field.

Abel pleased God and still witnesses to us concerning the meaning of real faith because he had the right attitude. Cain became the first murderer and was condemned to be a vagrant and wander the earth because he had the wrong attitude. Attitude makes all the difference!

But what exactly is the attitude that can make the difference between success and failure, between loving obedience and hate-filled envy?

I believe the attitude that makes the difference comes in three parts. It is the attitude that is:

1. Right with God.
2. Right with self.
3. Right with others.

The Attitude That Is Right With God

The attitude that makes all the difference is one that begins with God and understands the absolute need to be right with Him. You may have heard the old story about the three stoneworkers who saw their occupation from different perspectives. One said, "I'm carrying stone." Another said, "I'm building a wall." The third man said, "I'm building a cathedral to the glory of God!"

I have heard that story many times. Ironically, I had my own "stoneworker experience" during the summer between my freshman and sophomore years of college when I labored for a stonemason. First I would lift huge chunks of flagstone into a wheelbarrow and wheel them some two hundred yards to where the mason was building a wall. I'd dump the stone and then hustle back to mix more mortar so the mason could keep working. When I was hired, I was told the rules were simple: "Never let me run out of flagstone or mortar!"

What I especially appreciate about the Good News I

share with my congregation each week is that the attitude that can make a person right with God is made available through His grace. Scripture tells me I can do all things through Christ who strengthens me![5] Every Christian's walk of faith is built upon the foundation of Jesus Christ. All history—from beginning to end—is pointed to Jesus Christ. He is the center of history. He is the center of life itself.

In the next chapter I will concentrate more on how we relate to God and please Him, but right here I want to establish a fundamental point: *The attitude that makes all the difference starts with being right with God.* If you want to be right with God through Christ, start by saying, "I believe I can!" When I say, "I believe I *can*," it is my act of faith in "a God who *will*."

The Attitude That Is Right With Self

The attitude that begins by being right with God continues naturally into an attitude that is right with self. Lack of self-esteem is quite possibly the greatest problem in the world today. Ask any minister, psychologist, psychiatrist, counselor, judge, schoolteacher, police officer, or probation officer about his or her work, and in no time at all you will be hearing descriptions of people whose self-image is at zero or less. Poor self-esteem is one reason a young girl turns to prostitution, why a young man steals cars or pushes drugs.

Lack of self-esteem is often present when an insecure husband starts fooling around with other women to prove he is still "macho."

Lack of self-esteem causes countless people to lie, cheat, steal, take advantage, and care only for themselves. Lack of self-esteem paralyzes many people with fear and insecurity as it keeps them functioning at levels far below their potential.

Self-esteem—more precisely, the lack of it—spawns the

familiar story about the mother who was trying to get her son to get up and go to school. She patiently tugged and coaxed, saying repeatedly, "Come on, son, you've got to get out of bed and go to school."

But her son kept saying, "I don't want to get up. I don't want to go to school. It's boring and it's too hard, and besides that, nobody likes me. Why do I have to get up and go to school?"

Finally the mother got exasperated and said firmly, "Well, I'll give you three reasons you have to get up and go to school. First, it's the right thing to do. Second, you're forty-one years old. And, third, you're the principal!"

We smile at that old story but it contains a sobering truth. A lot of people don't want to get up and go to school, to work, or even to their Saturday golf game because they think life is too hard, it's boring, people don't like them, and they aren't worth much, so why bother?

No one feels more strongly about all this than my father, who wrote *Self-Esteem: The New Reformation*. In his introduction to this provocative and stimulating book, he defined self-esteem as ". . . the human hunger for the divine dignity that God intended to be our emotional birthright as children created in His image."[6]

I have learned from my father that any analysis of social or personal sins must take into account that at the core of our sinful or unsocial behavior is "a conscious or subconscious attempt to feed the person's need for self-esteem."[7] He writes:

What is "egotism"? It is a crass and crude attempt of self-esteem-impoverished persons to "prove that they are somebody." The truly self-esteem-satisfied persons are not "egotistic," they don't need to be.

Why is this need for self-esteem so all-consuming in individual behavior and so all-important? It is because we are made in the image of God! We are spiritually designed to enjoy the honor that befits a Prince of Heaven. We lost that position and privilege when our first parents divorced themselves from the Creator God.

Many years ago a classical student of the Scriptures, Matthew Henry, in his commentaries, noted on Genesis 3: "The immediate consequences of Adam and Eve's transgression: Shame and fear came into the world . . . they saw themselves disrobed of all their ornaments and ensigns of honor, degraded from their dignity, and disgraced in the highest degree, laid open to the contempt and reproach of heaven and earth and their own consciences."

How human beings handle that hunger for glory explains all psychological problems, all spiritual sicknesses, and all human sin. And this pitiful reaction to our personal need for divine dignity is profoundly pervasive.[8]

During the writing of *Self-Esteem: The New Reformation*, the famed George Gallup, Jr., conductor of the well-known Gallup Poll, was commissioned to do some research on self-esteem among Americans today. His pollsters discovered that people with a strong sense of self-esteem have the following qualities:

1. They have a high moral and ethical sensitivity.
2. They have a strong sense of family.
3. They are more successful in interpersonal relationships.
4. They view success in terms of interpersonal relationships, not materialistically.
5. They are more productive on the job.
6. They have a far lower incidence of chemical addictions. (In view of the fact that current research studies show 80 percent of all suicides are related to alcohol and drug addiction, this becomes terribly significant.)
7. They are more likely to get involved in social and political activities in their community.
8. They are more generous to charitable institutions and give more generously to relief causes.[9]

One significant statistic that surfaced during the Gallup Poll was this: Thirty-five percent of the Protestants had strong self-esteem, Catholics were about the same, and among the "other faiths," 40 percent demonstrated strong self-esteem.

Those who showed strong self-esteem were usually people who viewed God as a personal, loving, and forgiving being. They related to Him in a personal way. Those who simply went through ritualistic attendance at "typical" church services and had no more relationship to God than formal recitation of prayers, were more likely to struggle with gaining positive self-esteem.

Those of us in the church need to take seriously the words of Rene Dubos, one of this century's great sociobiologists, who writes:

> The most distressing aspect of the modern world is not the gravity of its problems: there have been worse problems in the past. It is the dampening of the human spirit that causes many people, especially in the countries of Western civilization, to lose their pride in being human and to doubt that we will be able to cope with our problems and those of the future.[10]

A familiar story that aptly illustrates Dubos' analysis describes the man who was peddling balloons on a New York street corner. He knew how to attract a crowd before he offered his wares for sale. He took a white balloon, filled it up, and let it float upward. Next he filled a red balloon and released it. Then he added a yellow one.

As the red, yellow, and white balloons were floating above his head, little children gathered around full of excitement and interest. A hesitant black boy looked up at the balloons and finally asked, "If you filled a black balloon, would it go up, too?"

The man looked down at the little boy and said, "Why, sure! It's not the color of the balloon, it's what's inside that counts."

"All well and good," you might be saying, "but how do I (or my spouse or my children or my friends) learn to

appreciate and be proud of what's inside? How does anyone build high self-esteem?''

I'll be talking a great deal about self-esteem throughout
this book, and everything I say will come back to the fact
that the human brain is a lot like a radio. To get the most
out of it, remember to do two things:

1. Stay plugged in.
2. Turn your dial.

To stay plugged in, remember who and what you are—
God's child, made in His image. As the late Ethel Waters
was fond of saying, ''God don't make no junk!''

To turn your dial, make your own decisions about how
you are going to feel or react. Remember the poem by Ella
Wheeler Wilcox I mentioned earlier in the chapter. Decide
that you are going to be happy today.

The Attitude That Is Right With Others

For the attitude that makes all the difference, you start
with being right with God, which gives you the power and
motivation to be right with yourself. As you turn your dial
to the positive, you find yourself tuning in other people
more often. In a word, you find yourself on their wave-
length! You see them as God's children—your brothers
and sisters.

One of the most dramatic examples of how right belief
can make you right with others is the story of Mom Schug,
who remained a member at Garden Grove Community
Church until she was in her eighties. Mom (her real name
was Bernice) was very close to our family.

When I was ten years old, Mom became the regular
babysitter for my four sisters and me, so my mother could
spend time during the day helping my father with his
ministry. For eight years, she arrived each day about 10:00
A.M. and stayed until late afternoon. When I got home

*I*t's not the
color of the skin,
but the *thoughts*
that live within.

from school, there was Mom Schug, a grandmotherly lady who loved all of us as if we were her own.

Mom passed away peacefully and swiftly, like a flower that had come to full bloom and was ready to drop its petals so the new seeds could sprout. Mom Schug lived the full cycle! Only a week before her death, she had been working at the Garden Grove Community Church 24-Hour New Hope Counseling Service.

Mom lived in a tiny mobile home that she had bought thirty years before. But every month she would take 10 percent of her social security check and place it in the offering plate at church.

People might think Mom Schug had a good life and few problems. The truth is, she lost her only son, Bob, in World War II. He enlisted in the navy so he could join the fight to end a horrible war. Bob was on a ship in the Pacific when he was struck in the leg by a shell. He was quickly taken below deck to the medics.

Doctors were preparing to amputate his leg when a kamikaze pilot on a suicide dive struck the side of the ship right where the medical center was, killing Bob, the medical team, and many others. What a crushing grief that was to Bernice Schug. But you know, God can take a crushing grief, and He can come rushing in! Mom Schug found a joy in her sorrow because she experienced the perfect love that comes from God.

Several years later, Mom received the bulletin from our church and saw that a former Japanese kamikaze pilot was going to be the guest on the following Sunday. She couldn't believe it! Days before he was to carry out his suicide plunge, the war ended. He went back to Japan and there he met a missionary and was introduced to Jesus Christ. Now he was traveling around the world, sharing his testimony of what Jesus Christ had done in his life. Mom Schug called my father and said, "Bob, I don't think I'll be in church this Sunday," and then she told him why.

"Well, Mom," he replied. "I can understand. You are human. If you don't want to come to church, then stay home and pray or read your Bible, or watch a church service on TV.''

Saturday came and my father received another call. "Bob," Mom Schug exclaimed, "are you sure you are going through with this?"

"Yes," he answered, "this man is a terrific Christian. He has a personal relationship with Jesus Christ." As she said good-bye, my father could hear her sobbing on the other end of the line. The next morning, the church was filling up fast, but Mom Schug came in the side door and sat in the back row. She had planned to sneak out before the service was over.

The service began with a few hymns and then the guest approached the podium. He shared a beautiful testimony and then closed with prayer. This was the time when Mom was supposed to have slipped out, but she forgot. By the time she opened her eyes to try to make an early exit, the Japanese man was standing only a few feet away from her. She could have left by the side door or gone down the aisle, but she didn't. Instead she walked over to the man, opened her arms, and embraced him. She whispered in his ear about her son and tears started streaming down both of their faces. When you've got love in your heart and Jesus Christ in your life, you can be right with others no matter what the problem might be![11]

One thing to remember about loving anyone—lovely or unlovely—is to beware of the power of negative ideas. A negative idea manifested at a moment of self-pity, jealousy, resentment, or anger or even a seemingly innocent moment of unkind thought that is harbored, nurtured, and acted upon, can be very destructive in its ultimate consequence.

There is a true story about a devoted pastor who counseled a woman suffering from a very rare, fatal disease. A secretary in the church saw them together and started a rumor that he was being unfaithful to his wife. The pastor could not defend himself without violating a pastoral confidence. When the woman died, the true story came out.

The church board and the pastor's family knew there was no foundation to that ill-fated rumor at all. Nevertheless, his reputation in the community had been demolished.

When the pastor discovered the source of the rumor, he called the secretary. In tears, she lamented, "I don't know how to apologize. What can I ever do to set things right again?"

"Here's what I want you to do," he replied. He gave her a pillow full of goose feathers and said, "Go to the high hill outside of town. When the wind blows, just let the feathers fly, and bring back the empty pillow."

"Oh, thank you," she cried. She went to the hill and scattered the feathers to the wind. When she returned, she showed the pastor the empty pillow and asked, "Now, can things be as they were? Will you forgive me?"

"One last thing," the pastor said. "Go back and pick up all the feathers."[12]

One of the best sermons ever preached in our sanctuary at Rancho Capistrano Community Church consisted of four brief lines quoted by our guest pianist of the morning, Roger Williams. It was a tremendous thrill just to have Roger, one of the world's fine entertainers, in our service. But it was a real serendipity when he concluded our 11:00 A.M. service by sharing something his own father often said:

> *There is so much good in the worst of us*
> *And so much bad in the best of us,*
> *That it hardly becomes any of us*
> *To talk about the rest of us.*

The Right Idea

In the eleventh chapter of Hebrews we find this definition of faith:

> Now faith is the assurance of things hoped for,
> the conviction of things not seen.

Scholars have found all kinds of deep truth in those words, but I think the deepest truth they communicate about living a life of faith is that attitude makes all the difference.

Everywhere I go people ask me how they can have more faith, deeper faith, real faith, etc., etc. I believe faith depends on your attitude—having the state of mind that impels you to be right with God, right with self, and right with others.

When Hebrews tells us faith is "the assurance of things hoped for," it speaks of an attitude that guides us in all our decisions and actions. I like the way one writer put it when he said real faith is really persevering—hanging tough, so to speak—to make the choices that are right and good.

No one can control my choice of attitude but me. No one can control your choice of attitude but you.

People can try to manipulate you. They can try to control you. They can try to put you down and make you feel bad. But in the final analysis, only *you* can make you feel badly. Only *you* can defeat yourself.

For years the world believed it was impossible to break the sound barrier. But test pilots like Chuck Yeager led us to new truths. For years the world believed it was physically and humanly impossible to run a four-minute mile. One man, however, chose to believe differently, and Roger Bannister broke the four-minute-mile barrier. Today it is broken every time world-class milers run.

For years no one believed it was possible to make a solo nonstop flight across the Atlantic, but Charles Lindbergh did it. Just a few decades ago the idea of a man actually walking on the moon would have caused derisive laughter, but people cheered instead of laughing when Neil Armstrong uttered his famous line, "One small step for man, one giant leap for mankind."

For its first fifty years or so, there was a belief that major-league baseball was for whites only. And then Branch Rickcy, the white owner of the Brooklyn Dodgers, invited

Jackie Robinson, a black third baseman, to turn baseball's dial.

Hundreds of thousands of myths, lies, and misconceptions have been proven wrong or changed because somebody had the attitude of faith that made the difference. A few years ago I wrote a short prayer that has helped many people to whom I've had the privilege to minister. I hope it helps you:

> *Oh, Lord, give me the self-esteem to believe in me*
> *And the vision to see where You want this child to be.*
> *Then give me the faith to carry it through*
> *And the wisdom to know I did it with You!*

Nobody Like Me

In all the world there is nobody like me. Since the beginning of time, there has never been another person like me. Nobody has my smile, my eyes, my nose, my hair, my hands, my voice. In all of time there has been no one who laughs like me, cries like me. And what makes me laugh and cry will never provoke identical laughter and tears from anybody else . . . ever. I am the only one in all of creation who has my set of abilities. There will always be somebody who is better at one of the things I am good at, but no one in the universe can reach the quality of my combination of talent, ideas, abilities, and feelings.

No one will ever look, talk, walk, think, or do like me. I am special . . . rare . . . and there is great value in me. God gave me my value. I need not attempt to imitate others. I will accept and celebrate my God-given differences. It is no accident that I am special. God made me for a special PURPOSE . . . and has a work for me that no one else can do as well as I . . . only one applicant for my job is qualified . . . that one is me. I am special because God made me special.

2

You Can Break
the Fear Barrier
—Now!

I LIKE COLLECTING golf stories. Somehow the tales of the golfer's woes and wiles apply to a lot of us, whether or not we play golf.

It seems a new convert went golfing with his pastor. On the very first tee he took a mighty swing with his driver and completely missed the ball! Now this man loved to golf, and whiffing his drive on the first tee was not his idea of having fun. He got so angry he wrapped his driver around the ball washer while muttering through clenched teeth, "I missed it! I missed it! How could I miss it?"

The man's pastor was shocked and looked very worried. "Now calm down," he told his new convert. "If you don't take it easy, the sky may part and the angel Zapula will zap you with a red ball of fire."

"The angel who?" asked the new convert.

"Zapula—he's the angel who's assigned to zap you every time you get out of line."

"I'm sorry, Pastor. I'll try to be more careful," said our friend, and they went on with their game.

Everything went fine for the next few holes. The new convert hit a particularly beautiful five-iron shot straight to the sixth green and was left with only a two-foot putt for a birdie. He steadied himself, took a deep breath, and stroked the ball firmly toward the cup. It looked as if it was going to drop for sure, but instead it just rimmed the edge of the hole and came right back out!

The new convert couldn't believe it. Then he couldn't stand it! He bent his putter over his knee, turned the air blue, and screamed, "I missed! I missed again! I missed again!"

His pastor calmly holed a ten-footer for a par, then came over and put an arm around his shoulder. "Come on, now, take it easy. You are really going to have to calm down or I fear the worst. I'm afraid Zapula will get you for sure."

"Hmm," said the irate golfer. "Funny you didn't mention Zapula when you told me about the Good News, but I'll try to relax."

They got through the first nine and most of the last nine holes with no problems. On the final hole, the new convert got ready to drive once more. *Have to stay out of the lake on the right,* he told himself as he got ready to tee off. *I'd better be sure I hook a little to the left—there's plenty of freeway over there to land in.*

He shifted his feet and hit what looked at first like his best drive of the day. But instead of sailing slightly left, the ball soared beautifully and majestically—right into the lake!

Now our golfer was really mad. He had no chance at all to win the match. His ball was gone and so was his temper. He marched out to where his tee shot had disappeared into the murky waters and threw his entire bag of clubs into the lake! Then he started ripping off his shirt so he could toss that in, too.

"Stop it!" cried his pastor. "I told you twice already. Zapula will get you if—"

Just then the sky parted, a red ball of fire came streaking down, and *Zap!* the pastor fell down dead!

The new convert couldn't figure it out. Zapula was supposed to get *him*—or at least that's what his pastor had said. Finally he heard some shouting. He looked up and saw Zapula jumping up and down, screaming at the top of his lungs, "I missed again! I missed again! I missed again!"

Some People Have the Zapula Complex

I like the Zapula story, not for its theology but for the choice bit of truth it contains. Zapula represents the caricature that a lot of people picture when they think about God. If they get too close or mess up too often, He'll zap them. At best, He'll put a black mark by their name, sigh, and say, "I knew it. I knew it. Never did think he [she] could make it."

I call it the Zapula Complex. People with the Zapula Complex fall into two main camps:

The first group doesn't want to bother with God much at all. People in this group say things like, "God? Who needs Him? He probably wants all my money—or at least He'll make me give up smoking. Besides, I'm not even sure He exists."

The second group is part of the church, but keeps its distance from God, so to speak. People in this group say in so many words that they believe in God but they don't want to get too close: "God is a very strict guy. I know I don't measure up to all of His rules and regulations. No point in getting Him riled. I can't please God anyway, so why get too chummy and risk getting zapped?"

Obviously, the Zapula Complex is no way to build a faith that helps you believe you can. What is the cure for the Zapula Complex? In Hebrews 11, the writer mentions many heroes of faith. We've already considered Abel, who faithfully obeyed God with the right kind of sacrifice and got bludgeoned to death by his brother, Cain, for his trouble.[1]

Next, we can read about Enoch, the shadowy figure who is mentioned in just seven verses of Scripture,[2] but what we do know about Enoch is impressive. Because of Enoch's tremendous faith, God allowed him to skip the formality of dying. He simply "took him up." One moment you could see Enoch, the next you couldn't. He was simply gone—taken home to be with God, who had already said how pleased He was with his life.[3]

How did Enoch please God so much? Obviously he didn't suffer from even a tiny Zapula Complex. What was his secret?

We get clues from the fifth chapter of Genesis, where we learn, among other things, that Enoch was the father of Methuselah, a rather famous biblical character because he had more birthdays than anyone else—969 in all. While Enoch lived on earth "only" 365 years, his life had a special quality because he "walked with God" and then he was no more.[4]

I've often been a bit frustrated by the lack of details on Enoch. What did he and God do on all those walks during those 365 years? How did he please God so much? Why did he get special privileges and get taken up (translated) into heaven without having to experience death? The answer seems to be *Enoch had faith.*

Without faith, says the writer to the Hebrews, it is impossible to please God, to draw near to Him and walk with Him. If you want to get to know God better, you must believe He is really there and that He rewards those who seek Him.[5]

To break the fear barrier, or any kind of barrier that may be coming between you and God, take three steps of faith. Believe that:

    God exists!
    God rewards!
    God cares!

*B*efore faith
can exist hope
must be born.

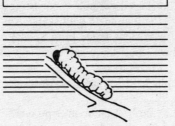

Start by Saying, "God, I Know You're There"

As I mentioned above, one kind of Zapula Complex contends that God isn't there—or at least we can't be sure, so why get too serious about Him? When we say we can't be sure about the existence of something, we usually mean it doesn't fit into the natural scheme of things. As the philosophers put it, we want empirical evidence—what we can experience by seeing, hearing, or touching.

God, of course, doesn't fit into nature's empirical evidence. He fits better in the realm called the supernatural—beyond nature. God doesn't fit in test tubes or on microscope slides. You can't even get Him on a videocassette.

It is most ironic that human beings have trouble with the idea of the supernatural. My personal conviction is that the most natural instinct of the human being is to believe in God. In fact, it is abnormal *not* to believe in God. When we look at the various cultures across the world, from the most primitive to the most sophisticated, we see human beings striving to get closer to God as they reach out to Him in all kinds of ways. It is as natural for the human being to believe in God as it is for the salmon to swim upstream or the swallows to return to San Juan Capistrano.

But while we are born to believe, we are a paradox. There is a God-shaped vacuum in our beings that only He can fill, but we still struggle with skepticism. We are like the little boy who came home from Sunday school, bragging about how good the class was. His mother asked, "What did you learn today?"

The boy replied, "I learned how Moses got the Israelites out of Egypt."

"How did he do it?" the mother prodded.

"It was very simple," the boy continued. "Moses hired some bridge experts and they built a suspension bridge ten times as long as the Golden Gate Bridge. It went clear across the Red Sea!"

"That's hard to believe," his mother laughed.

"Look," the persistent child said, "if I told you what they really taught me, you'd *never* believe me!"

Skepticism comes to most of us as naturally as breathing. Let me share one other story that illustrates what I mean.

The Japanese are famous for their skill with computers. Recently they installed a fully computerized scale in a huge airport. Instead of giving you a ticker tape readout of your height and weight, this scale gives you personal data via a mechanical voice.

A skeptical American dropped in a coin and out of the speaker of this inventive Japanese device came the following announcement:

> YOU ARE AN AMERICAN. YOU ARE 5'10" TALL. YOU WEIGH 185 POUNDS AND YOU ARE BOOKED ON FLIGHT 408 TO LOS ANGELES, CALIFORNIA.

The man was totally incredulous. He was sure someone was playing a practical joke on him. So he sneaked into a rest room, changed his clothes, put on a different coat, and pulled his hat over his ears so that it hid his face. Hobbling like a shrunken old man, the American stepped onto the machine, dropped in his dime, and waited for the announcement. It wasn't long in coming:

> YOU ARE AN AMERICAN. YOU ARE 5'10" TALL. YOU WEIGH 185 POUNDS AND WHILE YOU WERE CHANGING YOUR CLOTHES YOUR PLANE LEFT FOR LOS ANGELES.

Where Is the "Proof" for God?

Psychologists tell us that some people are just plain hard to convince of anything. They believe very little and trust practically no one. They employ what is called "manipulative avoidance reaction response.'' It is actually intentional inattention. They refuse to believe!

I've talked to people like that. They say they simply can't believe in God. Where is the proof?

Depending on the situation, I go through the various "proofs," but beforehand I explain that God can't be proven scientifically. You can't take His picture or measure Him with laser cameras. God is "seen" by faith, not through the cornea.

There are, however, several scientific principles or laws that strongly suggest God exists. For example:

The law of cause and effect certainly suggests a God behind it all. Go back far enough and you have to arrive at the "uncaused first cause." As the writer of Hebrews said, every house is built by someone, but God built everything.[6]

The law of entropy tells us the universe is running down. (Don't panic, we have several billion years to go.) The point is, if the universe is running down, it can't run by itself, under its own power. It had to begin somewhere, with Someone or something. That's what we talked about a moment ago: the mystical, *uncaused first cause!*

The law of design is one of the most convincing arguments for God I know of. Is all the design and order in the universe simply due to lucky cosmic accident? Why, for example, does the earth spin through space at 17,500 miles per hour? Why not 16,900 miles per hour? Why is the moon 240,000 miles away? Do you know what would happen if the moon were 50,000 miles away? The ocean tides would be so huge the water would wear down entire mountain ranges. Obviously owning beachfront property would be a thing of the past. In addition, there would be daily hurricanes.

The teleological argument (as the theologians call it) eloquently states that the design of the universe points to a Grand Designer. As the Psalmist said, "The heavens declare the glory of God; the skies proclaim the work of his hands!"[7]

The moral argument for God points out that all people across the face of the earth have a built-in sense of right and wrong. Where did that sense of right and wrong come from? Can you really account for it aside from Someone who created man and programmed him for right and wrong in the first place?

Finally, there is what the theologians call *the ontological argument,* which asks, "Where did we get our ideas of God in the first place?" How can man think of something that isn't there? Because we can conceive of God is a strong indication that Somebody gave us the ability.

We can go on and on with arguments for the existence of God. But in the final analysis we must take Him on faith. As I mentioned before, I believe that human beings are born to believe—born to believe in God. Fish were born to swim in the sea, birds were born to fly, animals were born to roam the face of the earth and man was born to believe in God.

Why didn't God create us in such a way that we couldn't help but believe in Him? Why does God require faith from us? After all, if there is such a Being as God, why doesn't He just prove Himself? I often hear that question.

We've already talked about a lot of the "proofs" for God, but nothing will finally and conclusively prove beyond all doubt that He exists. My father was talking with a group of Japanese people while attending an evangelistic crusade in Tokyo. He asked them what they called themselves, and they replied almost unanimously, "We are atheists."

"Why are you atheists?"

Their combined answer was, "We are very scientific. We do not believe in something that cannot be proven."

As if it came from his subconscious, my father heard himself saying, "That's a contradiction, for the truth is, when proof is possible, faith is impossible. If God proved Himself to us, we wouldn't be believers—we would simply be followers."

If there is a God, why doesn't He prove it to us? The

answer is simple: If He proved Himself to us (and it would be easy for Him to do just that), we wouldn't be believers—we would simply be followers.

I choose to believe God exists. In Him I live, move, and have my being.[8] Have you ever thought about what would happen if God took the day off? There is a story about an executive who came home from the office to find the house a total disaster. His wife was usually a wonderful housekeeper, so he simply couldn't understand why everything was such a mess.

"What happened?" he asked in amazement.

His wife looked up from the couch and said, "Remember how you always ask, 'What could you possibly be doing all day?' Well, today I didn't do it!"

If there is ever a day when God decides "not to do it," there will be a far bigger mess than the woman's unkempt house. To tell you the truth, I don't want to be around. In fact, none of us *will* be around. We will not exist because the very Source of our existence—God Himself—will be gone.

The Next Step: Realize God Rewards

While I have talked to my share of skeptics who hide their Zapula Complex behind sarcasm and "scientific bravado," I've also talked to a lot of other people who have no trouble believing God exists. Their problem (their particular brand of the Zapula Complex) is that they want to draw nearer to God but they are a little bit afraid (sometimes more than a little).

Hebrews says you have a good start toward pleasing God if you believe He *is*. Your next step is to relax and appreciate the fact that God never turns down anyone who means business with Him. He rewards anyone who sincerely seeks Him out. As J. B. Phillips says, He makes it worth our while![9]

How worth our while? Far beyond our imagining! Not

seeking God's best for your life is like settling for soggy cornflakes in cold milk from room service when you could go downstairs and enjoy a glorious buffet with dozens of entrées.

Room Service—at Any Cost

One summer, my sister Gretchen was traveling with my parents. They were all guests of a company where Dad was invited to speak over a several-day period. Their accommodations were in a lovely hotel that served one of the most elegant breakfast buffets known to man.

The first morning they were there, my father got up to take his usual run before breakfast. On the way back to his room, he saw the buffet table. It was glorious—piled high with everything imaginable: fruit, all kinds of meats, eggs, fish, blueberry and bran muffins, pancakes, waffles, and French toast. My dad had sworn off overeating, especially big breakfasts, but he couldn't resist and he decided to indulge on that particular morning.

When he returned to the room, he found my sister Gretchen cuddled up in bed, dozing peacefully. "Gretchen," he said, "come on out! Let's go down to breakfast!"

"Nope," she answered. "I'm ordering room service."

"Gretchen," my father asked, "do you know what you get here for room service?"

"Yes," she said, "breakfast in bed. I've never had breakfast in bed and today I'm going to."

"But Gretchen," Dad argued, "all you get from room service is cold cereal and milk."

"I like cold cereal and milk," she answered. "I want breakfast in bed."

"Gretchen," my father exclaimed, "you should see the buffet table! They have scrambled eggs—your favorite—bacon, French toast. . . ."

Gretchen pulled the covers over her head. She didn't want to hear it.

"Gretchen," he continued, "they also have blueberry muffins."

Gretchen pulled a pillow over her head.

"They have bran muffins and pancakes, too," Dad shouted as she buried her head deeper into the pillows and pulled a second blanket over her head. She didn't want to hear, because hearing meant changing her way of thinking. She would have to get out of a comfortable bed, get dressed, and go down to the dining room—something she just wasn't prepared to do.

It could well be that you are missing a super buffet—a literal banquet of love, joy, and peace of mind through a much closer relationship with Jesus Christ. All you have to do is make a few necessary changes. It may mean getting out of what you think is a comfortable bed, but it could be worth it. Dare to try something with God you have never tried before and see what happens!

One thing to remember is that God rewards those who *earnestly seek Him*. Maybe you need to draw closer to God while you are in conditions that don't match a posh hotel and a glorious buffet breakfast. Maybe you feel more as if you are in prison, captive to a lousy job or a boss who is a direct descendant of Simon Legree. Maybe illness has you behind its bars of pain. Whatever your "prison," God will reward your search for Him. He might even open the prison doors. That's what happened to Dr. Henry Poppen, who was on the staff of Garden Grove Community Church while I was growing up.

God, I Can Take No More! Open Up!

Dr. Poppen and his wife were guests in our home for Thanksgiving and other special occasions, and I shall not forget the way his eyes twinkled when we talked together. I consider him one of my mentors and a key influence in my life.

Dr. Poppen died at eighty-three. His distinguished ca-

eer of service to God included more than forty years as
ne of the first missionaries to go to China. During the
Communist takeover of China in the late 1940s, he was
called into public trial in the main city square. Over ten
thousand people jammed the square as accusation after
accusation was read against him. Finally, he was declared
guilty on all counts and told he must leave the country.

Dr. Poppen and his wife boarded a bus and headed to
Swatow, hoping to board a steamer and leave for freedom
in Hong Kong, and then travel back to America. But in
Swatow, Henry was pulled off the bus and placed in
solitary confinement. He was imprisoned in a cell six-feet-
by-eight-feet. The ceiling was so low, he couldn't stand up
straight. He didn't know what was going to happen to him,
but he did know that most missionaries who were prisoners
of Mao Tse-tung never lived to tell about it.

Mrs. Poppen was put on a train, then a boat, and finally
found herself in Hong Kong. She waited anxiously in a
hotel, not knowing where her beloved husband was.

Dr. Poppen spent hour after hour, day after day in his
small, dark cell. After four and a half days, he could stand
the blackness and the mental torture no more. At midnight
he got on his hands and knees by his small wooden cot and
prayed, "Oh, God, you know I am not Paul or John or
Peter. I am only Henry Poppen, and Henry Poppen can
take no more! Lord, open the door!"

He fell asleep on his hands and knees, only to be
awakened about an hour later by the creaking of the hinges
on his cell door. The guards came in and tied a rope
around his neck with a slipknot, ran it down his backbone,
and bound his arms behind him so tightly that if he struggled at all, he would strangle himself. Then they led him
down a dark, winding cobblestone street, until he saw the
reflection of light in rippling water. He heard the hum and
chunking of an engine. Then he saw the dark outline of an
ocean steamer, waiting with its gangplank down. The
guards shoved him onto the deck and said, "Now get out
of our country!"

The gangplank was raised, and the steam whistle blew. The captain took the rope off Dr. Poppen's neck and cut it loose from his hands. Dr. Poppen raised his head. God had heard his earnest prayer and had opened the door. He was a free man under God!

Was Henry nearer to God while in that intolerable prison cell, or was he closer after he was on the boat headed toward freedom? It's hard to say, but there is no argument with what Hebrews says: God ". . . rewards those who earnestly seek him."[10]

God, you see, has plans for each of us. The Old Testament prophet Jeremiah tells us:

> "For I know the plans I have for you," declares the Lord, "plans to prosper you and not to harm you, plans to give you hope and a future."[11]

Many of Us Need Our Eyes Opened

Do you want to draw closer to God? It's part of His plan for your future—a future filled with hope. As Hebrews puts it, all you have to do is open your eyes and see it out there ahead of you. Perhaps the Zapula Complex is clouding your vision. Your fears (okay, slight discomfort and nervousness) when around God keep you from seeing His plan and rewards very clearly. The Zapula Complex can be like the cataracts that closed the eyes of George W. Campbell at birth.

"Congenital, bilateral cataracts" they called it. "No known cure at present." George spent his childhood and most of his teenage years in darkness, but when he turned eighteen a new operation became available. He went through two long and risky surgeries on each eye over a period of six months.

George and his family kept praying and hoping. When the last operation was complete and the bandages were removed, the doctor asked, "George, do you see anything?"

All George saw was a dull blur, but then something happened. He heard a voice over his face saying, "George, this is your mother. Can you see?"

The blur turned into a color, the color took shape, and suddenly, for the first time in his life, George Campbell saw a human face. It was the face of a sixty-two-year-old woman, wrinkled, framed by white hair.

Much later in life, Campbell recalled, "It was the first face I ever saw—and was it ever beautiful!" He didn't see his mother's wrinkles. He didn't notice that her hands were gnarled and rough. They were the hands that had always held his hands. Hers was the voice that had spoken to him all those years. This was his mother.

Following his operations, Campbell lived a normal and beautiful life. He often said, "The most beautiful moment of my life was when my eyes were opened and I saw the face of my mother."

Many of us need our eyes opened to the possibilities God has for us. The most beautiful moment of any believer's life is when your eyes are opened and you see Jesus in a way you've never seen Him before. Maybe that's what you need right now. Maybe your Zapula Complex has you handicapped. Maybe you need to stop being a negative thinker, a bit wary or even afraid of God, and become a possibility thinker who discovers the potential of God's power within.

Staying in Shape Takes Consistency

It's your choice. You can draw closer to God than you've ever been before, if you sincerely want to. But it doesn't happen in a flash. It doesn't even happen over a six-month period. To draw nearer to God takes diligence. You have to be consistent and come to Him on a regular basis.

I see a close correlation between spiritual fitness and physical fitness. In my own physical-fitness program, my goal is to get in five workouts each week, alternating between an aerobics exercise class and a weight-lifting program.

My wife and I attend a one-hour aerobics class together, from 6:30 A.M. to 7:30 A.M. In this class our chief goal is to keep our cardiovascular system cleaned out by getting our pulse rate up to 120 beats a minute for at least twenty minutes. We also mix in several spot exercises to keep all our muscles toned. Following the aerobics class, we get back home in time for breakfast and a brief time of family unity and prayer with the older children before they leave for school.

My weight-lifting program is also one hour long, and I have a full routine of lifts, curls, and presses to keep my other muscles tuned and ready to go. I don't try for huge amounts of weight or a high number of repetitions, but I do try to be faithful in maintaining a schedule of four or five times a week in weight lifting or aerobics. With this kind of regular routine, I find that I stay in excellent shape. During periods when I get too busy and have to miss regular exercise, I quickly get sluggish and have less energy.

And it's the same with my devotional life. Coming to God regularly through prayer and the reading of His Word is part of what Hebrews means when it says that God rewards those who sincerely look for Him. You find God on your knees and in the Scriptures.

Yes, I know, it's possible to find God in the beauty of nature. You can feel God's touch as you fellowship with other believers. But the best ways to draw near to God are through talking with Him and letting Him talk to you through His Word and your meditation upon His thoughts.

Try it and see. Believe He is there. Seek Him out. Jesus Himself tells us how:

Ask and He will give.
Seek and you will find.
Knock, and the door will open![12]

The Best—or Second Best?

To believe in God is good.
To diligently seek Him is better.
To know that He is a God who cares is best of all!

Are you experiencing the best—or second best? You can attend any number of churches where there is no question that the preacher believes in God right down to the last verse of the Bible. And there is no question that he wants his parishioners to seek God diligently on a regular basis. When he doesn't think they are being diligent enough, he scolds and rebukes. He slaps wrists, hands, and sometimes faces with verbal barrages designed to create guilt, guilt, and more guilt.

I've often wondered why people take these verbal whippings Sunday after Sunday. Don't they want to walk out? How can they take it week after week?

Strangely enough, they not only take it but they also seem to like it. As they file out after the service you can hear them saying, "Great message, Pastor. God really spoke to my heart this morning!"

He did? If so, He didn't talk grace, He talked law. No wonder people have a Zapula Complex. They don't understand what the grace of God means! They think they have to earn their forgiveness and pay for their own sins. They like being verbally spanked because they think it will help them to not feel guilty anymore. They simply don't understand that Christ died on the cross and paid the whole price for their salvation once and for all. All they have to do is accept what He has already done!

In one of his books, my father wrote, "Man's biggest problem is that he hates himself. God's toughest job is to make you believe that you can be a beautiful person. Your most important decision is in choosing Him—choosing to accept God's forgiveness and choosing to take God into your life."

God practically shouts His message of grace to us. He isn't a Zapula cartoon figure hopping around complaining, "I missed again! I missed again!" He is your loving heavenly Father saying, *"I love you! I love you! I love you!"*

The question is, do we hear what God is saying to us? Are we tuned in to His care frequency? Or are we too busy doing all the talking?

Many of us are like the little girl who got to talk long-distance to her daddy on the phone. He wanted to tell his daughter how much he loved her, but he never got the chance because she talked nonstop about what she had been doing all day.

When she paused for breath, he made another effort to say, "I love you, honey," but she cut him off again with more eager chatter.

Finally, the father made one more valiant effort, but his daughter stopped him again. "Here, Dad, Mom wants to talk to you—bye—I'll see you soon," she said cheerfully, and was gone.

Is that a picture of your prayer life on occasion? Are you too busy talking to hear what God has to say? What He'd like to say is, "You aren't hearing Me. You aren't getting My message. I know you want to tell Me everything you've been doing to please Me, but it's by grace you are saved—through faith. It's My gift to you. Guilt trips won't do it. What counts is that I love you—no strings attached!"

Why Robin's Mother Could Forgive

Sometimes God's love speaks most eloquently out of tragic circumstances. In the fall of 1985, Robin Brandley, a student at Saddleback Community College, was brutally stabbed to death in the school parking lot. Police could find no clues whatsoever. She had not been sexually molested; apparently, the murderer struck her down as she was going to her car following an evening class.

Shortly after Robin was killed, I received a phone call from her father, who asked me if I would conduct a memorial service for Robin in our church. I agreed, and on the day of the service, the sanctuary was literally packed with students from Saddleback College who had come to pay homage to a classmate they loved a great deal. Robin was one of the most popular students on campus, president of several organizations, involved in many extracurricular activities, and a top student as well. But there was more to the emotional atmosphere in that service than Robin's popularity. As I gazed out into the young, attractive but grief-stricken faces, I was struck by the obvious love these young people had for Robin. The room was filled with it.

I had never met Robin, but it was very apparent she was the product of a loving home. As I brought the service to a close, Robin's mother indicated she wanted to come to the platform and say some final words. She came up the steps, supported on one arm by her husband and on the other by her son. Tall, stately, and immaculately dressed, this lovely woman stood in the pulpit and told the huge crowd of young people how much she and her family had loved Robin. She believed Robin would continue to live through the love she had spread during her life, and she hoped everyone there would live a life of love.

Then she said, "I forgive that person who took my daughter's life. What he did was not an act of love, for he did not know love. If he knew love, we would not have to be here today."

It is amazing what happens when love is in the hearts and minds of human beings. It empowers them to take a tragic negative and turn it into a wonderful positive. I believe that one of the primary messages of Hebrews 11 is that God rewards us as we earnestly seek Him, because nothing can stop God's love. One of the most beautiful rewards of salvation is the awareness of God's unconditional, undying, imperishable love. No matter what happens, He has a plan of infinite beauty and loving grace for your life!

Don't Lean Against the Wind

Let's look at that advice from Hebrews 11 one more time:

> Without faith it is impossible to please God, because anyone who comes to him must believe that he exists and that he rewards those who earnestly seek him.[13]

Do you really believe that? Or does Zapula still threaten you just a little bit? You can break that fear barrier once and for all—right now—by taking a bold new step of faith. You can relegate Zapula to his proper place: a myth, a joke, unreal, a lie. You can know the truth and be free from the fear that is coming between you and the One who loves you more than anyone in the universe.

I'm not talking about a leap into the dark or leaning against the wind. I'm talking about depending on solid rock and walking in God's light.

You have probably heard skeptics compare faith to a leap in the dark. But what do I mean by leaning against the wind? While a student at Boston University, a young man named Bill Stidger always walked to school early in the morning. His route took him past a skyscraper that was under construction. One morning he noticed a large group of people gathered at the foot of the towering network of girders that were forming the huge building.

"What's happening?" he asked a man with a hard hat who looked like a foreman.

"One of the workers just got killed," the workman replied.

"How did it happen?" Bill wanted to know.

"The fool," the foreman angrily answered, "was leaning against the wind!'' And then with tears in his eyes, he added, ''When I hired him last week I distinctly said, 'Don't lean against the wind!' ''

''What does he mean?'' Bill asked another hard hat standing nearby. ''What does he mean, *leaning against the wind?*''

''Oh,'' the other worker said. ''Here in Boston there is always a steady breeze in the morning. A firm, pressurized wind comes off the ocean and blows against the skeleton of this building. So when we work up there and move around on the girders, it's so easy to lean against the wind for balance. But about nine o'clock in the morning, the wind cuts off. And always without any warning! This new guy had just come from Indianapolis. He was used to working on a high rise, but he wasn't used to working in Boston. He was leaning against the wind, and when the wind cut off, he fell.''

Jesus was a carpenter who never built any skyscrapers, but He would have understood completely about leaning against the wind. In His most famous sermon, He talked about building your life on a rock, which can stand no matter what may happen. The rains may fall, the floods may come, and the *winds may blow,* but your life is secure because it's founded on the rock.

You Can Make the Ending Glorious

In this chapter we met Enoch, who had a three-hundred-year postgraduate course in understanding the difference between leaning into the wind and trusting solid rock. Twice in Genesis 5 we can read that Enoch ''walked with God.'' Before placing faith in Christ, our walk is likely to be away from God—self-centered, ignorant, and blind.[14] After we put our trust in Christ, we become new creations. The old walk is gone and the new walk with God's Spirit brings love, joy, and peace.[15]

Interestingly enough, God never forces us to walk with

Him. He's a gentleman all the way. If we want to draw near, it's our choice. Enoch made his choice and spent 365 years "walking with God." And in the end he walked right into heaven!

My father tells the story of taking piano lessons as a little boy. Grandma was his teacher and when he practiced for a recital, she was a stickler for going over the conclusion again and again. My father had to get that conclusion down perfect!

"Keep on practicing the conclusion, Bob. Learn those last measures!" she used to say. "Look, Bob, you can make a mistake in the beginning; you can make a mistake in the middle; the people will forget it—if you make the ending glorious!"

You can make the ending glorious! I don't know what kind of childhood you had. I don't know what kind of life you have had. I don't know exactly where you are right now! But wherever you are, Jesus is there, ready to reward your seeking and searching. He wants to put a gold medal around your neck. He wants you to have a good life. He is a God of reward because He loves you and wants to give you His very best. Take Him into your life—maybe for the first time, maybe in a new way that you've never tried before, but take Him. Walk with God and I can tell you the ending will be *glorious!*

Cures for the Zapula Complex

As I have worked with people who have a "Zapula Complex," I have seen the following verses work in their lives to help them relate to God in a more meaningful and comfortable way.

"I love those who love me; and those who diligently seek me will find me" (Proverbs 8:17).

"And you will seek Me and find Me, when you search for Me with all your heart" (Jeremiah 29:13).

"If we live by the Spirit, let us also walk by the Spirit" (Galatians 5:25).

Unfortunately, when we need verses like these the most, we don't always have a Bible with us. I urge those I counsel to consider memorizing key passages so they will have instant recall when needed.

3

Commit Yourself to Excellence

THERE IS AN old Indian story about a brave who went out hunting and found an eagle's egg that had fallen from its nest but miraculously remained unbroken. The Indian took the egg and put it in the nest of a prairie chicken. The eagle's egg hatched along with the other eggs in the prairie chicken's nest, and the little eaglet grew up with the other baby birds.

All his life the young eagle thought he was a prairie chicken. He learned to do what prairie chickens do: scratch in the dirt for seeds and insects, cluck and cackle and fly just a few feet off the ground with wings thrashing and feathers scattering to the wind. After all, that's how prairie chickens fly. They don't know any other way.

The years passed and the young eagle became full grown. One day he looked up and saw a magnificent bird high above in the cloudless sky. The huge bird seemed to hang in the air, borne by the wind currents, soaring with scarcely a beat of its huge, powerful wings.

"What a beautiful bird!" he exclaimed. "What is it?"

"That's an eagle—the chief of birds," somebody said. "But don't give it a second thought. You could never be like him."

The eagle might have died after living the life of a chicken, but fortunately he did give it a second thought. On another day, as he scratched in the dirt for seeds and insects, he looked up and again saw that same majestic bird as it soared high above, its huge wings outstretched against the sky.

Strange, he said to himself. *I, too, have giant wings and my feet have these huge claws that could be used for more than scratching the dirt.*

And so the eagle got a running start and leaped into the air, working his huge wings rhythmically and steadily as he had seen the huge bird do. Instead of rising only a few feet, as usual, he soared into the sky and found his true potential and destiny.

What made the difference? When the chicken-eagle got another glimpse of excellence as it soared past, high above, something clicked inside. He had always heard an inner voice whispering, "You can do more than this," but he had never responded. He had taken the advice of his chicken companions who said, "Why make more dust than necessary as you scratch your way through life? Settle for the status quo; it's safer than the wild, blue yonder."

When I share this story, I often tell audiences that we are all eagles in a chicken world. We have potential far beyond the status quo and mediocrity. As we look to God, we find our true identity. And as we find out who we really are, we begin to do and be what God designed for us.

The chicken-eagle story illustrates an awesome truth: *The person you see is the person you'll be.* You can commit yourself to the pursuit of excellence or you can settle for mediocrity. You can reach your real potential or be content with far less. As the famed psychologist William James put it:

Compared with what we ought to be, we are only half awake. Our fires are damped, our drafts are checked. We are making use of only a small part of our possible mental and physical resources.[1]

How You Can Escape the Mediocre

What does it take to get us to pursue excellence rather than allow the mediocre to bind and capture us? I think it takes at least two things:

1. A little wholesome fear of God—reverence for Him, not a Zapula Complex.
2. A lot of love for God—which translates into obeying Him because you want to, not because you have to.

As we have been making some discoveries about the familiar but mysterious concept called faith, we have looked at the lives of biblical people who have much to teach us. In chapter 1 we met Abel, who modeled the right attitude, and his brother, Cain, who modeled the wrong one. In chapter 2, we became better acquainted with Enoch, who demonstrated that the way to please God is by diligently seeking Him out and walking with Him in secure and satisfying trust.

Now I want you to spend a little time with another familiar figure in Faith's Hall of Fame as recorded in Hebrews 11. I speak of Noah, builder of the ark that kept the human race going after God got fed up with its evil ways and sent the Flood.

Unlike Abel and Enoch, we know quite a bit more about Noah. We have much more detail about how Noah acted in faith. I believe he presents an excellent model for pursuing excellence as well. Hebrews 11 tells us Noah pursued excellence by listening to God's warning and obeying His orders. The result? He saved himself, his family, and enough animals to get life on earth started again after a flood that destroyed everything. Noah's act of faith separated him from those who preferred to think as chickens. Noah became an eagle—an heir of the righteousness that comes by faith.[2]

Through his faith, Noah achieved the same state of excellence that is available to us today through the blood of Jesus Christ. He became right with God when he took Him at His word and acted on it. I believe that anytime we believe what God says and do something about it, we take a step of faith that commits us to pursue excellence.

There is a lot being written these days about excellence. Best-sellers such as *In Search of Excellence*[3] are devoured by presidents of great corporations and owners of the corner grocery. It's a tough world out there. Competition is fierce. Everyone is trying to make a buck and excellence seems to be the way to do it.

But what does excellence mean when you apply it to your own life? How does excellence fit in with having the power to grow beyond yourself?

And, just how do we commit ourselves to excellence and then pursue and obtain it?

Excellence—Not Perfection

One reason some folks get discouraged or turned off by all the talk about excellence is that they think pursuing excellence means they must be perfect. And because they can't achieve a flawless state, why try to be excellent?

Excellence, however, is not a state of flawlessness—always being letter-perfect, impeccable, faultless, immaculate, pure and untainted to the last molecule. Excellence is being the best you can be and doing the best you can. For any believer, excellence starts with taking God at His word and doing His will.

Noah did, even when it looked as if he had lost his mind. Think about it. Noah received God's totally outrageous weather forecast and started building a giant ark, smack in the middle of a desert where it didn't rain often enough to float a rowboat, much less a ship over four hundred feet long. Noah wasn't perfect but he was obedient.

Noah has much to teach us. God doesn't sit in the heavens with calipers and stopwatch demanding that we be perfect. (Yes, I know Jesus told His followers to "be perfect," and we'll be looking at what that means in chapter 9.) What God does want is your obedience because then He can turn your negatives into positives, your defeats into victories, and your failures into successes.

I like Ted Engstrom's advice:

> Develop your own style. No one has had the life experiences you have had; no one has the contributions to make that *you* can make. So it's not a question of being better than someone else. Excellence demands that you be better than yourself.
>
> Some people are outgoing, while others are introspective. Some are thinkers rather than doers. Some are leaders; some are followers. Some are ahead of their times; many are behind. Some are musical geniuses; most are not. Some are great preachers; many are not. But whatever category you are in, right now you can make that single, deliberate move toward a life of excellence.[4]

I especially like what Engstrom says about being "better than yourself." In today's dog-eat-dog, win-lose world, the message is loud and clear:

> "Be better than the other guy—when you get him down, don't let him up."
> "Go for the jugular."
> "Winning isn't everything, it's the only thing."

Dr. Denis Waitley, best-selling author and specialist in behavioral psychology, has been a guest on the "Hour of Power" television broadcast. Dr. Waitley travels the country, often speaking to Fortune 500 executives to share his positive philosophy of self-esteem and being a winner, which he has explained in books such as *The Psychology of Winning, The Winner's Edge,* and *Seeds of Greatness.*

Before the 1984 Olympics, Dr. Waitley served as Chairman of Psychology on the U.S. Olympic Committee's Sports Medicine Council. He and others on the council spent long hours working with Olympic athletes, giving them tips on improving their performance, from a physical standpoint, of course, but probably even more important, from a mental and emotional standpoint. Dr. Waitley writes:

> In the words of a U.S. Army commercial, we tried to help our Olympic performers "be all that they could be." If they won the Gold, great! If they finished well back in a pack of thirty or forty, also great, as long as they gave it all they had, and could say they had reached down deep for as much excellence as they had in them.[5]

Dr. Waitley believes that a look at the history of the Olympic Games shows they were founded not on the principle of "getting all the Gold you can," but on the ideal of "being all you can be."

The Apostle Paul (who some think may have written the letter to the Hebrews) was a dedicated sports fan who probably was a spectator at athletic competitions in cities like Corinth. Paul sums up the biblical definition of excellence quite nicely when he says, "And whatever you do, whether in word or in deed, do it all in the name of the Lord Jesus, giving thanks to God the Father through him."[6] Better than anyone, Paul knew the answer to our next question:

Why Is Excellence That Important?

Maybe you've heard or seen the attitude that seems to say, "After all, nobody's perfect, why should we be excellent? God's grace will get us through—He always understands when we miss the deadline, forget the appointment, or fail to reach the goal—again."

So why be excellent? Why do your best? Because we owe our best to God and we owe our best to ourselves. God's grace is not a permission slip to wallow in mediocrity.

We owe our best to God because He has given His best to us. Remember Enoch, the man who "walked with God"? The Bible says Enoch pleased God so much he didn't have to die—God just took him.[7] Then in Genesis, the story of Noah tells us he was a righteous man, a good citizen, and that he also "walked with God."[8] Obviously, Noah enjoyed the same kind of relationship with God that Enoch had.

So, when God came to Noah with the news that He was going to send floodwaters to destroy the earth and orders to build a gigantic boat, Noah didn't file a long list of objections or reasons he couldn't do the job for at least six months. He and God were friends. Noah simply went to work doing "everything just as God commanded him."[9] After all, when God is (A) your creator, (B) your constant companion, and (C) your good friend, you owe Him your best shot, not a halfhearted effort.

To bring all this up-to-date, it's not hard to see that we have even more reason to give God our best shot. He has given us His best in Jesus Christ. Theologians often cite the parallel between Noah, who was saved through the ark, and the Christian, who is saved through Christ's sacrifice on the cross.[10]

What Do You Do With 50,000 Incorrect Bibles?

But what happens when you seek to honor God with your best and error creeps in—a very big error? That happened once when the "Hour of Power" television broadcast printed 50,000 copies of *The Possibility Think-*

er's Edition of the New King James Version of the Bible, published by Thomas Nelson Publishing Company. It was a beautiful piece of work, bound in genuine leather, dyed blue, with the spine embossed in silver.

There was only one problem: One tiny letter of one tiny word was an error. And that tiny error reversed the meaning of an entire sentence that taught a great truth and turned it into a great lie. The sentence was supposed to read, "With our faith in God, we can do all things." But imagine for a moment what happens when you take the *r* out of the word *our* and change it to a *t*. The sentence then reads, "With out faith in God, we can do all things."

And so 50,000 copies of *The Possibility Thinker's Bible* were ready to teach readers that they could do all things without having faith in God! One wrong letter in a word seems like a small problem, but it was actually a very big problem. What would we do with these 50,000 somewhat less-than-excellent copies of the *Possibility Thinker's Bible?*

Excellence can always find a way. We turned that particular scar into a star by taking every single Bible and correcting it in pen and ink by hand. Dedicated (and skilled) volunteers simply painted out the erroneous *t* and printed in the correct letter *r*. The Bibles were saved and became collector's editions!

Why go to all that trouble for one small letter? Why bother with a verse that the vast majority of readers would never notice, and if they did, would they even care?

The answer was as simple as the solution was difficult: You don't knowingly put out something as precious as God's Holy Scriptures when the printing contains an error that completely contradicts His teachings. In your pursuit of excellence, you always owe your best to Him.

The pursuit of excellence is also worthwhile because you owe your best to yourself. I'm not talking about self-centeredness. One wrong letter in 50,000 copies of *The Possibility Thinker's Bible* made them all useless because it placed emphasis on self instead of on God. But when you commit yourself to excellence, you commit yourself to doing God's will, which is the only real means of lasting fulfillment and genuine satisfaction.

A Different Kind of Cure for Depression

Striving for excellence is the bottom rung of that ladder we all climb toward self-esteem—building and keeping a positive self-image. In chapter 1 I quoted from my father's book *Self-Esteem: The New Reformation*, in which he suggests that the reason every human being has such a deep need for self-esteem is that he or she is made in the image of God.

God has designed us for self-fulfillment. When we go about obtaining self-fulfillment the right way—through doing His will—we find peace, joy, and happiness. But when we try to go the self-centered route of egotism, commonly called the ego trip, we end in cynicism, despair, and depression. The Director of the National Institute of Mental Health, Dr. Bertram Brown, has called depression the number-one problem facing the United States today. He stated:

> We have to make a frontal attack on the feeling of helplessness that's causing depression in our country today. Depression costs the United States of America five billion dollars a year in direct hospital and drug costs. We have no way of calculating how many more multiplied billions of dollars it costs our country in indirect costs, such as broken families, alcoholism, drug addiction, and welfare payment to people who have become emotional cripples.[11]

Dr. Brown went on to say that one of the best ways to battle depression is to give people success experiences that help them realize their lives are not helpless or hopeless. And what's the best way to achieve a success experience? By pursuing excellence with enthusiasm!

There is always a risk involved. We'll be looking more closely at daring to take risks in the next chapter. But you can pursue excellence and reach it—if you are willing to make the effort. And you can have success and more self-esteem if you are willing to take the risk.

If you think small, your self-esteem will remain small. Some questions for each of us to answer are, "What am I doing with the ideas God sends my way? Am I developing them to the best of my ability, or am I squelching them, ignoring them, or rejecting them? Is my self-denial and humility a cover-up for my laziness and mediocrity?"

A favorite fish of many hobbyists across the world is the Japanese carp, known as the koi fish. The fascinating thing about the koi fish is that if you keep it in a very small tank, he will grow no bigger than two or three inches. Move him to a larger tank or a small pond and he will reach six to ten inches. Put him in a very large pond and he can get as long as a foot and a half. Put the koi fish in a huge lake where he can really stretch out, and he will reach sizes up to three feet. I have visited Japan and have seen koi fish that were three hundred years old and were well over three feet long.

You're probably well ahead of me and already thinking, *Okay, I see the point. The size of the fish is in direct relation to the size of the pond.*

And in that truth there is a fascinating principle that relates to ideas. Little ideas that fall into little-thinking minds produce little achievements. But when those same little ideas drop into big-thinking minds, they become enormous achievements! Just as the size of your thinking determines the growth of your ideas, the size of your thinking determines the growth of your self-esteem!

Why is striving for excellence important? That's like asking why breathing fresh air and eating good food are important. Without them, a person functions at a fraction of his real capacity. No wonder some people look as if they are half-dead. They live in a high rise, fight their way to work every morning through smoke and exhaust fumes, get no exercise, and eat junk food that clogs their arteries, corrodes their stomachs, and ties their intestines in knots.

You can destroy your self-esteem just as easily as you can destroy your body by feeding your brain the junk food of small, warped ideas that keep your self-image shrunken and emaciated. But you don't have to be a victim, you can be the victor. Take Paul's advice:

> Whatever is true, whatever is noble, whatever is right, whatever is pure, whatever is lovely, whatever is admirable—if anything is excellent or praiseworthy— think about such things. . . . And the God of peace will be with you. [12]

How Do You Search for Excellence?

If we believe that in its ultimate sense excellence is doing God's will, then the best way to start our search is to seek God's fellowship earnestly and obediently, committing ourselves to a faith that is sure of what it hopes for and certain of what it does not see.

The search for excellence can include numerous challenges and disciplines. I think especially of three ways to "be" excellent:

Be creative.
Be positive.
Be humble.

Be creative. Erich Fromm once said, "Most people die before they are fully born. Creativeness means being born before one dies." [13]

I believe Fromm wasn't talking about creative genius or the talents of a gifted few. I believe he meant you and me as well. Not everyone can compose a complete symphony at age four. Not everyone can paint the *Mona Lisa* or write *Hamlet*. But all of us can have what Ted Engstrom calls

". . . a *creative attitude,* an attitude that says, 'I am willing to be fully born, to abandon the secure certainties of life, and to part company with my many illusions. I will live a life of faith and courage, even if it means aloneness and being different.' "[14]

If that isn't a perfect description of Noah, then the swallows don't spend their summers in Capistrano! In today's jargon, Noah had it made. He had a fine reputation among his fellowmen, and at the same time he was called a righteous man who walked with God. When God gave Noah the news of the impending Flood and orders to build an ark, Noah didn't hesitate. He abandoned the secure certainties of life, dropped everything he was doing, and started building a giant boat with no blueprints, no computer, not even a Skil saw. All Noah had were his primitive tools, some gopher wood, and God's instructions, which left him room for quite a bit of creativity:

> "Construct decks and stalls throughout the ship and seal it with tar," God told Noah. "Make it 450 feet long, 75 feet wide and 45 feet high. Construct a skylight all the way around the ship, 18 inches below the roof; and make three decks inside the boat—a bottom, middle, and upper deck—and put a door in the side."[15]

That was it. No details or specifications on how high to make the decks or how wide to make the stalls. No measurements on how big to make the door on the side (or any tips on how to keep the ship from leaking). Just, "Make a boat out of gopher wood. . . ."

To add fuel to any frustrations Noah might have felt, he had to build the giant ship in the middle of the desert, hundreds of miles from any body of water. Talk about living a life of faith and courage even if it means being alone and "different"! Can't you see the neighbors walking by, whispering to one another, "There's old Noah, working on his ark. Says a flood is coming. A flood! Poor fellow! The light is on but there's nobody home."

Thanks to Noah, mankind got another chance, and ever since there have been those who pursue excellence with the creative attitude, "Let's try something different, even if people think it's a little nutty."

What? A Church in a Drive-in?

I think of my own father, Robert H. Schuller, who came to California with my mother in 1955 with five hundred dollars in his pocket and instructions from the Reformed Church of America to begin a ministry in Orange County. The only problem was that he didn't have any money to build a church and couldn't find any public place to rent for use as a worship center.

Dad finally settled on the Orange Drive-in Theatre and planned to make the tar-paper roof of the snack shack his pulpit area. As soon as he got an okay from the drive-in theatre manager to use the theatre on Sunday mornings, he put out what he calls his "first immodest public announcement":

IN THREE WEEKS WE WILL BE STARTING WHAT WILL BECOME ORANGE COUNTY'S NEWEST AND MOST INSPIRING PROTESTANT CHURCH. COME AS YOU ARE IN THE FAMILY CAR!

Reactions from church leaders in the community weren't long in coming:

"What? A drive-in church? Never heard of such a thing!"

"Hear you're going to have to begin in a drive-in theatre. You poor fellow. How unfortunate that you couldn't find some empty hall."

My dad, who had already developed the concept of "Possibility Thinking," was bombarded from every side by impossibility thinkers.

A "friend," who was also a minister, dropped by for a visit and said, "What's this I hear, Bob? You really aren't planning to start a new church in a drive-in theatre, are you? Why, that place is nothing but a passion pit."

Dad tried to remind him that the Apostle Paul had preached to pagan philosophers on Mars Hill and that "wasn't such a holy spot." His friend was unconvinced, however, and spent two more hours trying to talk my father out of his idea. He left after giving a priceless demonstration of how an impossibility thinker thinks. He warned my father that his new church couldn't possibly work and that his decision was a terrible mistake.

My father admits he wavered a bit at that point but recovered by remembering a verse of Scripture from Paul's letter to the Philippians that was especially meaningful for him at that moment: "Being confident in this one thing, that God, who has begun a good work in you, will complete it."[16]

On the Saturday night before the first service was to be held, Dad went out to the garage and checked the trailer which held the mahogany organ he and Mother had hauled all the way from Iowa, as well as offering plates, pulpit Bible, microphone, and even a raincoat and umbrella. Back in seminary, my father had committed himself to a vision of excellence when he did a paper on George Truett, who built one of the great Baptist churches in America. Later, as a young pastor considering a move to California, Dad had what he calls a "positive possibility thought":

THE GREATEST CHURCHES HAVE YET TO BE ORGANIZED.

Dad had his motivation. He had his vision of excellence, and if he had to start on the tar-paper roof of a snack shack in the Orange Drive-in Theatre, then he would do just that!

The first service was held as planned on March 27, 1955, at 11:00 A.M., with fifty cars, around one hundred people, and $83.75 in the offering. From that humble but creative beginning came the Crystal Cathedral, one of the modern-day wonders of the world, a national TV ministry reaching millions every Sunday, and missionary efforts encircling the earth.[17]

Be positive. No search for excellence will get very far with a negative attitude. If my father had listened to his clergyman friends, Southern California's first drive-in church would not have sprung up among the orange groves to reach thousands, and later millions, with God's message.

If Noah had listened to the jibes and jokes of his neighbors, he could easily have been overwhelmed by the immensity of his task. And even after he completed the ark and maneuvered everyone and everything on board as instructed, there was the interesting question, "Who gets to clean up this mess every morning?" Noah not only needed to be positive but he needed a sense of humor as well!

Is Your Input Positive or Negative?

A few years ago the Stone-Brandel Center in Chicago, Illinois, conducted an experiment to learn the results of negative versus positive thinking. The leader of the experiment was Dr. Lacy Hall, who believed that people are the product of what comes into their lives, especially the thoughts that come into their minds each day. A large number of persons were recruited for this study, and each individual was asked to keep a diary of his or her daily life by recording everything that came to mind. One goal of the study was to discover what percentage of input into the human brain in the course of a day was positive and what percentage was negative.

For eighteen months, the participants in the study dutifully recorded everything that came to mind each day. Their diaries began with the opening of the day. If they turned on the television set, they had to write down exactly what they watched. Whether it was a newscast or a talk show, they logged it into their diaries and noted whether the input was positive or negative.

If they worked or had to go out during the day for any

other reason, every encounter had to be recorded, whether positive or negative. If they listened to a radio station, read a certain newspaper or book, visited with family or friends, participated in any kind of entertainment, or went to church, everything had to be documented.

After a year and a half, Dr. Hall and his staff collected, calculated, and computerized, under controlled research conditions, all of the data in the diaries of the study participants. The results were startling.

For the most part, the people who kept the diaries ended the experiment feeling discouraged or depressed most of the time. But is it any wonder? Most of these diaries recorded 90 percent negative input. Only 10 percent of the thoughts and concepts that came into the lives of the study participants during that year and a half were positive!

There were a few people who had a high percentage of positive input, but they were rare. For the most part, these were people who had unique relationships in marriage, in the office, and at home. And they also had connections with outstanding positive-thinking churches.

But on an overall average, the entire group of study participants had 75 percent negative input from life over an eighteen-month period. Dr. Hall's summary of this study observes that everyone is fighting against tremendous odds. The average human being who is trying to be positive is fighting a losing battle, unless he's associated with something unusual that constantly feeds him positive thinking which results in positive emotions.

Is it any wonder that so few people seem to take to the road that leads to excellence? They are stalled before they start by the negative thinking that bombards them from every side. If you want to pursue excellence, start by taking this tiny step: Do, say, or experience at least one positive thing each day. A second step is to try to increase the positive input into your mind whenever possible as you decrease the trash, junk, and banality wherever you can. You can't eliminate the negative in your life—you can only dilute it with the positive.

The positive thinker finds something good in every situation, and it often helps his creativity as well. I love the old story about a young man named Woolworth who opened a new store—a brand-new business of his own. As he prepared for his grand opening, a merchant down the street got a little nervous about this young man taking some of his business away, so he ran an ad in the local paper:

> DO YOUR LOCAL SHOPPING HERE. WE HAVE BEEN IN BUSINESS
> FOR FIFTY YEARS!

Young Woolworth couldn't believe it! How could he handle this competition? What should he do? The next week he countered with an ad of his own:

> WE'VE BEEN IN BUSINESS ONLY ONE WEEK—ALL OF OUR
> MERCHANDISE IS BRAND-NEW!

Do all you can to be a positive possibility thinker. Remember Babe Ruth. If he had let his 1,330 strikeouts get him down, he would have never hit 714 home runs!

Be humble. The virtue of humility is not always associated with excellence. A popular line of thinking is that being humble means you have to be looked down on, defeated—a loser. True humility, however, is not the mark of losers but of winners. Obviously, Noah had humility or he couldn't have given up his position of "big man in the community" and started a project that soon had him labeled "the village idiot." Noah was humble enough to do what God told him. *Noah put his own pride and reputation aside to get the job done.* For me, two other outstanding examples of humility are Albert Schweitzer and Abraham Lincoln.

Am I Willing to Carry Wood or Wash Boots?

Albert Schweitzer's ability to humble himself by deserting a brilliant and highly successful musical career to go back to school and become a medical doctor is impressive enough in itself. And Schweitzer didn't stop there. He took his medical degree and buried himself in darkest Africa, where he spent the rest of his life in the crudest conditions treating people who could pay little or nothing.

Despite a lack of money, Schweitzer managed to build a hospital in the African jungle. One day he asked one of the natives to carry some wood. The native, who had been learning to read and write, replied, "I'd like to, sir, but it's beneath my dignity. I am a scholar, an intellectual."

Albert Schweitzer chuckled and said, "I've always wanted to be an intellectual, too, but I never quite made it. So I'll carry the wood!" And he did just that.

Stories of Lincoln's humility are legion, but one I like best concerns a visit made by Lincoln and his secretary of war to the battlefield home of General George McClellan, commander of the Union forces at the height of the Civil War. They waited in the parlor of McClellan's home for the general to return from the front.

Finally the door opened and in walked General McClellan. He saw the president and secretary of war but never acknowledged them. Instead, he walked by them and on up the stairs to his room. Lincoln and his secretary assumed McClellan would be down very soon, so they continued to wait. When the general did not appear, they sent the maid to inquire. She returned and said, "I'm sorry, Mr. President, but the general asked me to tell you that he is tired and has gone to bed."

The secretary of war was shocked and said, "Mr. President, that's unacceptable. You must relieve him of command."

Lincoln thought about it for a minute, then said, "No, I will not relieve him; that man wins battles. I would hold his horse and wash the dirt from his boots if he could shorten this bloodshed by one hour.''

Every now and then I ask myself, "How humble are you, Robert? Would you carry the wood or wash the dirt from someone's boots to get God's work done? How hard are you willing to work to be excellent?"

John Gardner has written a brilliant book with the simple title *Excellence*. In that book he says:

> Some people may have greatness thrust upon them. Very few have excellence thrust upon them. They achieve it. They do not achieve it unwittingly, by "doin' what comes naturally"; and they don't stumble into it in the course of amusing themselves. All excellence involves discipline and tenacity of purpose.[18]

What is excellence? In the final analysis it is doing God's will.

Why is excellence important? It is our only means of true fulfillment and satisfaction.

And how do we commit to a life of excellence and pursue it?

"Quick," said the man as he excitedly jumped into the taxi, "Do you know how to get to Carnegie Hall?"

And the cabby replied, "Practice, man, practice."

Is It Your Time to Fly?

On the edge of the ledge an eaglet stands,
The time has come to fly.
For that mighty bird has a destiny
And so, my Lord, have I.

As the eagle is not content to stay at levels safe,
So I, on the edge of the ledge
Await Thy will.
Lord, I was meant to fly.

*G*reat things
grow from small
beginnings.

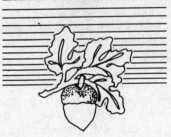

4

Dare to Live by Faith

So FAR WE have talked about three steps of faith in our study of how to "grow beyond ourselves":

Developing the right attitude, which starts with being right with God, goes on to being right with self, and naturally flows into being right with others.

Breaking the fear barrier, or what I call the Zapula Complex, which keeps us avoiding God, afraid and nervous to be around Him because He might "zap" us for our mistakes and imperfections.

Committing our lives to excellence, becoming the best we can be to the glory of God.

Now I think you are ready for a dare—in fact, it's going to be a triple dare, because it has at least three parts. Did you ever have anyone dare you when you were a kid? I remember spending summers with my cousins on their farm in northwest Iowa. The hayloft of the huge barn was practically empty at the beginning of summer, with only

66

few bales of hay left after feeding the livestock all winter.

My cousins would stack the hay bales and create a platform from which they would swing on a long rope tied high in the rafters of the barn. As they swung clear across the hayloft and back, their feet would dangle more than twenty feet off the floor.

I was the "city slicker" to my cousins, and they would dare me to try their swing. The thought of being that high in the air on the end of a rope was terrifying to me and I always refused—at first. But my cousins continued to dare me to the point where I could no longer resist.

I would climb to the top of the stack of hay bales, throw myself to the mercy of the rope, and sail out into space, squealing with delight as I swung from one end of the barn to the other. If the rope had snapped or my grip had slipped, I could have broken a leg or worse, but I had been dared, and I had to do it.

What does it mean when you have been dared? What are the dynamics behind, "I dare you"?

I believe that to be dared is to be called to go into action. All of a sudden, everything is on the line: your reputation, your ability to back up what you've been saying.

"I dare you" is a call to authenticity. You have to come through. It's a matter of, "Act now or forever bite your tongue."

Those times when some other kid dared you to do something, what happened if you shrugged it off or gave some clever excuse that seemed to get you off the hook? More often than not, you got a "double dare" and there you were, faced with another make-or-break situation.

Suppose, however, you came up with an even more ingenious answer to the double dare than you did to the original challenge? (Sometimes it's amazing how fast you can think when you have to.) You thought you were out of the woods when—there it was—the triple whammy. Some-

one *triple dared* you to put it all on the line and stretc
yourself as you had never stretched before.

That's what this chapter is all about: a triple dare, so
speak, to:

> Put yourself on the line and stretch a
> little further to live by faith.

Are you willing to accept my dare? Maybe you're n
quite sure. Let's look at that word *dare* a little harder. Th
four letters in D-A-R-E give us a thought-provoking acro
tic that sums up what I believe the dare is all about:

Decide
Act
React
Elevate

Taking a dare means you *decide* to do something. The
you put your decision into *action,* but you're not throug
yet. Most important, perhaps, is that you are ready to se
what happens and to make necessary corrections or change
in order to succeed. You're ready to *react* and as yc
react, you change, you progress—you *elevate* to a plac
beyond where you were before.

So, unlike childish dares which were often silly or eve
dangerous, I believe any worthwhile dare should be d
signed to help you grow, stretch, change, mature. That
just what I have in mind when I say, "Dare to live b
faith!"

God Dared Abraham and Then Some

As we look into the book of Hebrews, we find mar
people who took God's dare to live by faith, but standir
head and shoulders above them all is Abraham. In fac
Abraham went down in history as the man who was jus

fied by faith,[1] and became the father of the Hebrew nation, the man through whom all nations of the world would be blessed.[2]

As we look at Hebrews 11, what can we learn about how Abraham reached the top of the list in Faith's Hall of Fame? We see that he did at least three things:

First, Abraham acted when God called. He simply picked up his belongings and left, "even though he did not know where he was going."[3] Abraham was a man of action. When God said, "Move," he moved!

Second, Abraham believed God's promise that he would be the father of many nations. We have to go back to Genesis to see what God offered Abraham in exchange for leaving his country, his people, and his father's home:

> *I will make you into a great nation*
> *And I will bless you;*
> *I will make your name great. . . .*
> *and all peoples on earth*
> *will be blessed through you.[4]*

Would that have been enough to convince you to go? It was enough for Abraham. He didn't ask God for a road map from AAA and a report on traveling conditions. He didn't have any map at all. He just took off, at the age of seventy-five, with his wife, Sarah, his nephew, Lot, his belongings, and his servants, to head west toward the land of opportunity.[5]

Abraham was short on questions and long on belief—not a bad way to live if you are interested in a life of faith.

Third, Abraham was willing to obey. The Bible has no more vivid example of obedience than Abraham's willingness to sacrifice his only son, Isaac, at God's command. Put yourself in Abraham's shoes for a minute. You and your wife were childless well past the age of ninety. At that age, having children is out of the question. Somehow, "through faith," you had a son. Things are going great but all of a sudden God says, "Take your son, whom you love, and go sacrifice him on the mountainside."[6]

Now, it's one thing to move lock, stock, and camel herd from one location to another when God calls. It's another to think you're hearing God say, "Okay, it's time to kill your only son, the one you had to have so much faith to produce in the first place."

Genesis doesn't tell us anything about Abraham's reaction. It just says that early the next morning he packed up and left with two servants and his young boy, Isaac.[7]

Was Abraham bluffing—or stalling, perhaps—hoping God would change His mind?

Somehow Abraham had faith in what God had said to him earlier. He trusted God completely. God had told him that through his descendants all nations would be blessed. How could that be if his only son were sacrificed? Scripture says Abraham reasoned that God could raise Isaac from the dead, if necessary.[8]

God was making things difficult for everyone—including Himself! Nonetheless, Abraham obeyed, right up to the final seconds before he was to plunge the knife into Isaac's chest. At that moment the angel of the Lord called a time-out, so to speak, and told Abraham to stop, that his act of obedience proved his faith and reverence for God.

Now there was no doubt about it. Abraham was the one. All nations on earth would be blessed because Abraham was obedient.[9]

Problem to Solve or Decision to Make?

No wonder Abraham is the supreme example of faith in the Bible. He repeatedly had problems, but he always responded by daring to decide to do something about those problems.

Can you picture it: When Abraham left his home in the Chaldees (present-day Iraq) to head west to Canaan (present-day Israel), somebody probably called out, "Take care!" I believe Abraham responded something like this: "Take care? I think it's time to take a chance. God has told me what He wants. Now I have to do it. People who take care don't go anywhere."

Plenty of problems awaited Abraham, but he had made one decision and was ready to make more. Decisiveness is a necessary characteristic of a life lived by faith. Most of us really don't have problems; we have decisions to make:

- If you're an employer and you're having problems with an employee, you have a decision to make.

- If you're an employee having problems with your employer, you have a decision to make.

- If you're a spouse having problems with your husband or wife, you have a decision to make.

- If you have a bad habit, if you have a hang-up, if you can't forgive someone who has slighted you, you have a decision to make.

Almost every problem continues to remain a problem because of fear to make a decision.

As I was growing up, I was taught not to "take care" but to take charge and take a chance. I learned that my problems weren't problems at all—only opportunities to see the possibilities and make decisions that could lead to progress and success.

I also learned that life is a series of decisions we make as individuals, as persons made in God's image. And the way we see ourselves as human beings will determine the decisions we make and the way we govern our lives.

As I mentioned in the Introduction, I once had the opportunity to visit the five-acre estate of one of the finest film actors of all time, Gregory Peck. He shared with me the story of how he purchased his beautiful home:

People who "take care" don't go "anywhere."

I was in the middle of filming the life of General Douglas MacArthur. We were working on a deadline and I was very busy. I had no idea my wife had decided to go shopping for a home. On that particular morning we were going to film the scene in which MacArthur would address both houses of Congress. Six hundred hired extras were on hand to play congressmen and senators who would listen to my "old soldiers never die, they just fade away" speech. I put the finishing touches on my eloquent lines, straightened my full-dress uniform, and prepared to shoot the scene. Just then I was called to the phone. It was my wife.

"Honey, you've got to get down here. I've found our dream house," she said excitedly.

I said, "What dream house?"

"The dream house we've been looking for all our lives. You know what I'm talking about. You've got to come down here and see this house. It's on the market and it already has a couple of offers on it, but we've got to have this house. You've got to get down here."

I tried to say in a very sweet tone, "Darling, you have to realize that I'm about to shoot a scene. We have six hundred hired extras. The set is prepared. I have to be here all day shooting. I cannot leave."

"But honey," she said, "you've got to come."

"Not really, darling. You've got to understand the picture. I am in full-dress uniform and I'm playing General Douglas MacArthur. My hat has all the stars across the front. My lapels shine in the light with all of the fruit salad and medals. I am literally General Douglas MacArthur. I'm too busy to come and look at a house."

"But honey, you've got to see our dream house or we're going to lose it."

I could tell my wife was in no mood to be turned down, not even by General Douglas MacArthur. So I finally worked out an hour for lunch and took the studio limo over to the address she had given me.

I arrived in full-dress uniform to view the dream house, the house I had always wanted. I strode onto the property in full-dress uniform. As far as anybody who really didn't know me could tell, I was General Douglas MacArthur.

"Where's the Realtor?" I said. "'Show me the property."

I walked around the estate for six minutes, never looked inside, then said to my wife, "Buy it. I don't care what it costs. Buy it." And then I was gone.

The irony of it all is that I'm terrible at making decisions. I take forever to make a decision and I made one of the biggest decisions of my life in six minutes. I have a feeling it had to do with the uniform.

In uniform or out, how we see ourselves will affect how we make decisions. You can see yourself as a general or an admiral, or you can keep telling yourself, "I'm only a buck private" or "I'm only a seaman third class."

When you see yourself as a child of the King of kings, and Lord of lords, you will begin making the right decisions for your life.

The way to start is to say, "Yes, Lord, I love you. Yes, Lord, we make a good team. Yes, Lord, lead me in the paths of righteousness and I will have no fear because I know You are with me."

When you can see yourself in the full-dress uniform of the child of God, your problems will start to dwindle. You will see them as decisions you have to make and you will be ready to dare to make those decisions because you know God is with you.

Not to Act Is Not to Decide

Harvey Cox has observed, "Not to decide is to decide." I would like to suggest that to decide and then not to act is not to decide at all.

Decisions must be followed by action or they die. The number-one killer of decisions is procrastination. Once you decide, don't fumble around the way the young man did after having a wonderful evening with his new girlfriend.

He had never kissed her, and he thought to himself, *What's the matter? Are you afraid? I dare you to do it!*

So at the door, he said, "Can I have a kiss?"

She just shifted a bit, so he said, a little louder this time, "Can I have a kiss?"

She shifted around a little bit more, so he got a little bit closer and said a little louder, "Can I have a kiss?"

She just looked at him, so he said still louder, "Can I have a kiss?"

By that time she was almost nose-to-nose with him and he just couldn't figure it out. So he said, exasperatedly, "Are you deaf?"

She replied, "Are you paralyzed?"

Just as the young man was paralyzed by fear (was it really indecision?), we can be immobilized if our faith is feeble, our desire is diluted, or our will is a little wimpy. In the last chapter, we saw that if you want to commit to excellence you have to act—you have to do something about achieving excellence.

Every believer is called to excellence. In the Gospel of John we find Jesus telling His disciples that if they have faith, they will be able to do what He has done and even more than that. "Ask me for anything in my name, and I will do it."[10] You have Jesus' word on it. He will answer the prayer that asks, "Lord, help me fulfill the commitment to live my life by faith."

Faith Is a Verb, Not a Noun

And so you make a commitment and go forward with action. You go forward with faith because faith is not a noun, it is a verb.

When faith is a noun, it is dead. It becomes a religion that binds and restricts us from doing the will of God. But when faith is a verb, it gives us the means and the ability to walk the way God wants us to walk and live life in His power.

I often ask people in my congregation, how many are formerly Presbyterians? How many are from a Catholic background? What about the Methodists? the Baptists? the Nazarenes? the Assemblies of God? And, oh yes, we can't forget the Episcopalians or the Lutherans or any number of denominations, including my own, the Reformed Church of America, the oldest Protestant church with an unbroken ministry in the United States.

Fifty-four Dutch colonists, all members of the Reformed Church in the Netherlands, bought Manhattan Island in 1626, built a Dutch windmill, and held worship services in the loft. Today that same church is Marble Collegiate Church in New York City.

Why do I mention all these denominations? Because denominations are a good example of how faith can be a noun or a verb. Too often denominationalism turns faith into a noun. Members of some churches simply go through the motions, protecting the status quo, never taking any dares and never achieving excellence.

It really doesn't matter to what denomination you belong or if you're in any denomination at all. What does matter is that your faith is a verb, not a noun. When faith becomes a verb in your life, it frees you to pursue excellence, to take dares, and to do greater things than you ever thought possible. Through the blood of Jesus Christ we are cleansed, purified, and brought to a state of rightness with God. And through faith in Him, we can do far more than we ever dreamed possible.

When faith is a verb, it becomes action based upon the assurance of things we hope for and our conviction of things we cannot see.

Action Always Leads to Reaction

When I was small, my father and I would play with a big rubber ball. I remember him bouncing it on the ground and using our playtime to get in a little teaching as well:

"Life is like a rubber ball," he'd say. "What you give will come back to you." Then he'd bounce the ball off the ground or the wall and catch it on the rebound for emphasis.

I would often think of what he had said when I played my own version of handball with my friends. We didn't have a professionally designed court, with lines and boundaries. We would simply bounce the ball against the garage door and try to land it in a little square we had chalked on the driveway. Whoever missed the square lost points; whoever hit the square gained them.

Our simple little game was based on the same principle my dad taught me: "For every action there is a reaction." Every time we hit the ball, it bounced off the wall and came right back.

Now that I'm an adult, I see the action/reaction principle at work many times a day. Life *is* like a rubber ball. What you give comes back to you. What you throw out comes back to you. Then it's time for you to react.

Whenever you dare to make a move or take action, life may bounce back at you. You'll never know if you've made the right decision unless you act upon your decision and see what happens.

No matter who you are, how good you are, or how smart you are, you're bound to make a wrong decision sometime. Fortunately, whether our decisions are right or wrong, we always have the chance to react. We have the chance to adjust, to learn, to change. We have the chance to make it right, to make up for what we did or didn't do. When life bounces back, we have to be ready to react. The question is not, *"Will* I react?" The question is, *"How* will I react?"

If we trace Abraham's experiences, we find him making good moves and bad ones. For example, when he and his family reached Canaan, a famine struck and they had to travel to Egypt to get food to survive.

Pharaoh, the Egyptian king, saw the beauty of Abraham's wife, Sarah, and he told Abraham he wanted Sarah for himself. Abraham feared for his life. The result was several deaths in Pharaoh's household due to diseases God sent in judgment of Pharaoh's act. In short, many of Pharaoh's people died because Abraham lied.

When Pharaoh confronted Abraham, the great man of faith admitted he had lost his nerve. He didn't want Pharaoh to kill him (which he probably would have done if Abraham had told him that Sarah was his wife), and so he lied to save his skin. The result was that several other people died instead. Abraham got out of Egypt with his life and his wife, but it was a black mark on his record.[11]

Abraham returned to Canaan with his entire family and he and his nephew, Lot, proceeded to become wealthy in livestock, silver, and gold. About that time the herdsmen who worked for Lot started quarreling with Abraham's herdsmen. If the two families stayed together, it was obvious there just wouldn't be room for both of them in that particular neighborhood.

This time Abraham was ready. Instead of arguing, he suggested they part company. To prove his goodwill he gave Lot the choicest territory while he took second best. God blessed him for that and renewed the covenant He had made with Abraham, assuring him that he would make his offspring "like the dust of the earth."[12]

Through trial and error, Abraham learned to be adaptable. When dealing with problems, adaptability is an invaluable trait. Two stories I especially like show how someone solved a problem by adapting to a situation and coming up with a creative reaction.

A Short History of the Ice-Cream Cone

During the 1904 World's Fair held in St. Louis, Missouri, a vendor in a hot-waffle booth ran out of paper plates on which he was serving his waffles. He was dismayed to learn that no one else in the exposition would sell him any plates to replenish his supply. All the other vendors were hoarding their inventories, trying to make as much money as they could for themselves.

A nearby ice-cream vendor expressed delight over the waffle vendor's plight. "That's the way the old waffle crumbles," he remarked. "It looks as if you would be better working for me selling ice cream." The waffle vendor couldn't see that he had an alternative, so he agreed to buy some ice cream from the ice-cream vendor at a discount and resell it at his own booth, dishing it up in small cups.

As the waffle vendor tried to recoup his losses by making a small profit selling ice cream, he continued to think about what he could do with all the waffle batter ingredients in which he had invested most of his savings in order to capitalize on the huge attendance at the St. Louis World's Fair.

He had made decisions, all right, and he had acted. But his plans weren't working. How would he react to this problem? Suddenly, an idea struck him like a bolt of lightning. Why hadn't he thought of it before? He was certain it could work.

At home the next day, with the help of his wife, the waffle vendor made a batch of one thousand waffles and pressed them thin with a flat iron. While they were still hot, he rolled them into a circular pattern with a point at the bottom. The next morning he sold all of his ice cream before noon and all one thousand waffles, with three different toppings, as well!

How did he do it? By putting scoops of ice cream in the cone-shaped waffles. As a result of running out of plates, he had been forced into inventing the "ice-cream cone."[13]

How the Hot Dog Was Born

A similar "necessity is the mother of invention" story happened in the 1930s. A German immigrant in Philadelphia was trying to make a living selling knockwurst and sauerkraut in a small restaurant. Because of the Great Depression, times were hard, and he was unable to afford plates and silverware. So he developed inexpensive cotton gloves for his patrons to wear while they held the knockwurst, draped it in sauerkraut, and then ate it.

A major problem arose, however, because his customers took the gloves home with them to use for gardening and other odd jobs around the house. He nearly went broke trying to maintain a supply of cotton gloves.

To solve the problem, the creative immigrant split a German roll down the center and placed the knockwurst and sauerkraut in the opening. As he served his customers the next day, he explained to them that the split bun was taking the place of the serving gloves.

As one of the customers tried the new roll with the knockwurst in the middle, he looked over and saw one of the restaurant owner's dachshunds snoozing in a corner. Normally there were two dachshunds, but the other was not in sight. The customer quipped, "Now we know why you're trying to cover up your knockwurst in that fancy roll. What happened to that other dog you used to have?"

Everyone laughed, but in that instant the "hot dog" was born![14]

When we act, life may throw us a curve. Then we have to react. We can react with flexible creativity or we can freeze up, blow up, or try to lie our way out. As usual, God dares us to do the right thing, to react the right way. And when we do, He takes us to higher ground, and that brings us to our final point in the word D-A-R-E.

The Purpose of It All: Elevate!

Why take a dare from anyone, even God? Your primary reason should be to glorify Him. Taking a dare shouldn't be an ego trip; it should be a journey toward maturity and growth. That's why the *e* in our dare acrostic stands for

"elevate." God has called us into the Kingdom of His
dear Son by His grace.[15] Once we are in the Kingdom,
He has further plans for us. He has further work for us to
do. He wants us to grow, to mature, to reach higher to our
full potential.[16]

Whenever you take God's dare to step out in faith, you
are in for tough times. Deciding will be tough. Acting on
your decision can be even tougher. When the rubber meets
the road you have to react, possibly change course, reevaluate, and maybe go back to square one. But when you
finally reach your goal you will know the joy of elevation.
You will know the fulfillment of climbing a bit higher on
the trail God has marked out for your life.

You may be wondering, as I have often wondered, "Do
I have what it takes to react to difficulties and discourage-
ment and go on to higher ground? Is my faith strong
enough?"

The late Corrie ten Boom told the story of how as a
child she went to her father and shared her fear: "Papa, I
don't think I have the faith to handle real trouble. I don't
know what I'd do if you should die. I don't think I have
the faith that some people have to face trouble."

Corrie's father looked at her tenderly and said, "Corrie,
dear, when your father says he will send you to the store
tomorrow, does he give the money to you today? No, he
gives it to you when you are ready to go to the store. And
if you are going on a train trip and need money for a
ticket, does your father give you the money when we
decide you may take the trip? No. He gives it to you when
you are at the depot, all ready to buy your ticket. Corrie,
God treats us the same way. He doesn't give you the faith
until you need it. When you do need it, He will certainly
give it to you."

Corrie never forgot her father's words, and later her life
became a testimony to their truth. As she faced horror after
horror in a German concentration camp during World War
II, God always gave her the faith she needed to make
decisions, to act on them, to react to incredible pressure

and persecution, and to elevate, to find new heights of spiritual progress, even in the hell of Ravensbruck.

Have you reached your full potential? Are you daring to even think about it? What does God have out there ahead of you to help you discover what is deep within yourself? What is He daring you to try right now?

In the farthest reaches of northern Alaska there is a spot called Glacier Bay that is as primitive, virginal, and un-spoiled as it was at the dawn of Creation. There are no cars, houses, or neon lights. If you tour Glacier Bay on a cruise ship, you will sail beneath a three-hundred-foot-high cliff of diamond blue ice that creaks and groans and sud-denly splinters from top to bottom. With a screeching crack and a deafening snap, a huge chunk of this millennia-old glacier will slide thunderously into the ocean and explode in white foam. The echo of the explosion will reverberate through the hills of the desolate countryside and bounce off the ship on which you travel.

Many geologists feel certain that, as this river of frozen ice scoured the bottom and sides of the valleys through the centuries, it carried with it vast, unknown amounts of precious metals. Within that mountain of ice at Glacier Bay may be the largest, purest gold nugget that has ever been created! It simply hasn't been uncovered yet!

Could there be a gold nugget deep within you that you haven't yet discovered? You will never know until you take God's dare to decide, act, react, and elevate. God created all of us so that we might elevate to be in union with Him, to glorify Him, and enjoy Him forever. That's our purpose for living!

The gold nugget waiting for discovery in your life may not be any tremendous accomplishment such as developing a corporation or building a church. It may have nothing to do with success that can be measured by a computer or a TV news camera. But none of that is where your real nugget lies anyway. Your purpose for living is to be one with God; to grow to that point where you are face-to-face with Him and you can hear Him say, "I love you."

The Apostle John wrote a letter to the Church at Ephesus and said, "Dear friends, now we are children of God, and what we will be has not yet been made known. But we know that when he appears, we shall be like him, for we shall see him as he is."[17]

The Bible tells us our lives are like tender plants. Eventually, we fade and are gone. Life is but a fleeting moment, but eternity with our Creator is waiting.[18]

You may have heard it said that God has a wonderful plan for your life and that it's a plan for good and not evil.[19] I'd like to think that He has a wonderful "dare" for your life and it's a dare for your good, your prosperity, your joy and happiness. To take that dare you must first make the decision to love God, and then to elevate, to climb and grow, step-by-step, to become the new person God wants you to be.

A Roughrider's Dare

It is not the critic who counts: not the man who points out how the strong man stumbled or where the doer of deeds could have done them better. The credit belongs to the man who is actually in the arena; whose face is marred by dust and sweat and blood; who strives valiantly; who errs, and comes short again and again, because there is no effort without error and shortcoming; who does actually try to do the deed; who knows the great enthusiasm, the great devotion, and spends himself in a worthy cause; who, at the worst, if he fails, at least fails while daring greatly.

Far better it is to dare mighty things, to win glorious triumphs, even though checkered by failure, than to take rank with those poor spirits who neither enjoy much nor suffer much, because they live in the gray twilight that knows not victory nor defeat.

Theodore Roosevelt

5

Learn the Secret of Success

IT WAS ONE of the proudest moments of my life.

"You made it!" exclaimed my father, as we met outside following my college commencement ceremonies.

"Yes," I replied with a big smile, "I made it, and it was tough!"

"But it was worth it, wasn't it?" my father boomed enthusiastically.

"It was worth it," I agreed, "but I have to admit that at times I wondered. It was quite a hassle."

My father looked at me and his eyes were drawn to the tassel swinging from my graduation cap. He touched it lightly and said more softly, "The tassel is worth the hassle."

Leave it to my dad to come up with just the right phrase to put a great truth into unforgettably simple form. Suddenly the struggle of the last four years seemed insignificant. The tassel was worth the hassle—and then some!

"You bet!" I laughed. "Not bad for a guy who graduated from high school not even knowing how to read!"

84

It was true. I did graduate from high school barely able to read. As a little fellow, I had said to my father, "Boy, Daddy, I'd like to be a preacher when I grow up—just like you!"

My father had said, "Bobby, if you pray every night and say, 'Lord, help me to be a preacher when I grow up,' it can happen."

And so every night I prayed my standard "Now I lay me down to sleep . . ." prayer, followed by requests of God to bless Mommy and Daddy and everyone else I could think of. Then I would close with, ". . . and Lord, help me to be a minister when I grow up."

I continued to pray that prayer, right up into high school, but unfortunately my desire to be a minister wasn't matched by a natural love for books and studying. As I entered my sophomore year, I realized that in order to become a minister, I had to get some education. I would have to graduate from high school, go on to spend four years getting a bachelor's degree in college, and after that there would be four years of seminary!

Did the magnitude of my task inspire me to start hitting the books with a fresh new commitment to excellence? Not exactly. Being a sophomore in high school, I had my own solution to the problem. I didn't like reading, and seldom read anything on my own except *Car and Driver* and *Road and Track*. I hated being called on to read aloud in class because I struggled through many of the words and phrases.

Although I never cracked a book in high school, I still graduated with little trouble by using a two-part strategy:

First, I listened very carefully in class and took a few notes to remember the things the teacher believed were important. Second, when test time came, I grabbed one of the smartest students in the class and quizzed him: "What do you think will be on the test tomorrow?" He'd tell me, "Oh, probably this and this and *I know* she'll ask us *that*. . . ."

"Oh, *really?*" I would say, as if I had somehow missed reading about those important items. "What was that again? The important dates in the Civil War are on page one eighty-eight, you say?"

And so with what I gleaned by listening in class and what I could get from talking with the A students just before test time, I got through high school with a B– average! My only problem was that my study habits in high school came back to haunt me when I went on to attend Hope College in Holland, Michigan. I quickly discovered that college wasn't high school. Listening carefully during lectures and doing some verbal cramming by talking to the A students just before exams doesn't work with college profs who delight in creating monster reading lists that must be covered in a few weeks' time.

Now I was in trouble! I had dared to try college without proper preparation and now I had to react, and fast. The bottom line is that I learned how to read in a hurry! I learned that you can't really take any shortcuts in your educational process, because sooner or later it will all bounce back at you. You have to pay the price sometime, and I paid dearly with countless nights of poring over books and writing papers.

If my older sister Sheila hadn't helped me, I doubt that I would have made it. She was also attending Hope at the time and would often tutor and help me in other ways. She was especially good at spelling and usually went over all my papers to correct misspelled words before I turned in my assignments.

I recall a single-page report that I had laboriously typed out, double-spaced, looking up every word I wasn't sure about. Sheila wasn't around and couldn't check it for me. It came back with sixteen spelling errors clearly marked in red ink!

Yes, college was a hassle, but I kept going and finally got that tassel.

My college experience taught me something else that proved true as I continued on through four years of seminary and two years of internship to finally enter the ministry. I discovered that no matter how much education you get, it doesn't end because you walk across a commencement platform and receive that much-coveted diploma. A diploma on the wall doesn't signify that *now* you are educated. Your whole life is an education, and in one sense, receiving a diploma is not the end of your education, it's only the beginning!

No matter what occupation we choose, life always has another "final" or another "term paper" just around the corner. There is always another deadline, always another assignment of some kind. The corporate world has a phrase for doing a good job on a report, a presentation, or a project: "Nice going. You did your *homework!*"

It seems as if homework will always be with us.

Sometimes as you do that homework you may fail or fall short, but you keep going. You keep at it when your arms are tired, your legs are weak, your feet hurt, and your eyes are red with stress and strain. If you want to succeed, you learn from your mistakes. You learn that life's ups and downs and twists and turns are your real education, and you never stop going to school.

Have you ever watched a professional golf tournament on television? Sometimes everything comes down to the eighteenth green and the final putts by the two front runners. You hear the announcer saying, "Well, let's see how Nicklaus does with his putt. He has the same line as Palmer did when Arnie missed to the left. Jack went to school on Palmer's putt, so let's see if he plays the break a little better."

As good as pro golfers are, they "go to school" on one another, watching their opponents' failures and trying to capitalize on their mistakes in order to win the match.

Moses Never Stopped Learning, Either

In the life of faith, school is never out. To be sure of
what you hope for and to be certain of what you cannot yet
see, you never stop learning and growing. That is a major
message we find in the life of Moses, one of the true men
of faith in the Bible. It is easy to see why he made Faith's
Hall of Fame in the eleventh chapter of Hebrews. Outside
of Jesus Himself, Moses is perhaps the most admired and
most discussed personality in all of Scripture.

Moses' life was an educational experience from beginning to end. Long before he was born he was on a colli-
sion course with overwhelming responsibility. Hundreds of
years before Moses' time, Joseph, the great-great-grandson
of Abraham, predicted the Exodus of the Israelites from
Egypt.[1] It fell to Moses to lead that Exodus according to
God's timetable, but in order to be the leader that God
needed, Moses had to be prepared—he had to be educated.

Moses' story began in a gruesome way. His people, the
Israelites, had spent some four hundred years in Egypt and
had grown in such numbers that Pharaoh, the Egyptian
king, began to worry. "These Hebrews could become too
many for my soldiers and overthrow us," Pharaoh told
his people. "We'd better make them our slaves, and for
good measure, start killing off some of their newborn boy
babies."

That was the kind of world into which Moses was born,
and to save his life his mother hid him for three months.
When she could hide him no longer, she executed a desperate plan. She put her tiny son in a basket and floated it in
the reeds of the Nile River, in a carefully chosen spot near
the palace of the Egyptian king.

As she hoped, Pharaoh's daughter came down to the
Nile to bathe and found the baby in the basket. Moses'
sister watched from a distance while all this went on and
then just "happened by" to ask Pharaoh's daughter if she
would like one of the Hebrew women to nurse the baby for
her.

"Yes," Pharaoh's daughter answered. And, of course, back ran Moses' sister to get Moses' mother to be the nurse!

Unaware that she was becoming the victim of one of the classic "stings" of all history, Pharaoh's daughter instructed the Hebrew woman who was brought to her to nurse the baby she had found. And so the woman (Moses' mother, Jochabed) took the baby, nursed him, and brought him up in his early formative years. Scholars believe Moses may have been able to live with his real family until he was at least three years old, and possibly until he was twelve.

Scripture tells us that when Moses "got older" his mother turned him over to Pharaoh's daughter so he could live with her as her "son." There in Pharaoh's palace, Moses received the finest education available. He graduated "magna cum laude" from his formal education, so to speak, but God had more learning planned for him. As Moses would learn, his formal education barely scratched the surface; God had his "real" education planned in an eighty-year postgraduate course![2]

From Moses' long and incredible career we can learn why and how education is the key to success. How does education become a key to succeeding in life?

1. Education gets us started.
2. Education keeps us going, because it never really stops.
3. Education draws us closer to God.

Education Gets Us Started

The story of Moses' miraculous delivery from death to be reared in the courts of Pharaoh himself shows us two things: First, Moses was educated for a particular purpose and for a particular reason. But more important, we see a very particular direction in his life.

I believe God has that kind of direction for every individual. You and I were born with a specific and particular goal. Before we were born, the mind of God had created a plan for our lives—a system of education, if you please—which would be tailor-made for us and us alone.

"There was nothing so special about my education," you might be saying. "I went to Central Grade School, graduated from South High, and got a couple of years in at Northeast J.C. What's so special about that?"

I admit that may not sound too special on the surface, but don't forget that life has been teaching you much more than you ever learned in your "formal education." God allows the trauma and tribulation, the difficult and stretching times in your life. For people of faith, these difficult times become courses of study that are part of a quality education which advances them toward their purpose in life. What is your purpose? You can find out through prayer and seeking God's guidance. You can discover your goals and your purpose for life. You and God can work it out.

Your Education Will Keep You Going

Plato probably thought himself profound when he said, "The direction in which education starts a man will determine his future life." Most mothers, however, are way ahead of him. They know by instinct that the way their children get started in life is the way they will go.

There is a story about a little boy who angrily stormed home from his first day in kindergarten. "How did you like school?" his mother asked gently.

"I didn't like it," he replied sulkily. "In fact, I not only didn't like it, I'm quitting!"

"You're quitting!" his mother exclaimed incredulously. "Why, you can't do that!"

"I don't care if I can or I can't," said the little boy. "I'm quitting."

"Why do you want to quit school?" his mother probed.

"Look, Mom," he said, "school is an awful place. I can't write. I don't know how to read. And they wouldn't let me talk. There's nothing to do, so I quit!"

Naturally, that mother made her son go back to kindergarten and try it again. Eventually, he did learn to read and write and they did let him talk sometimes.

It doesn't matter how your education starts. Mine started rather poorly, due to my own laziness and a school system that let me get away with it. But when my college professors came down on me with the kind of pressure I had never seen before, I used my weak start as a springboard and went from there. I had good skills in observation and memorizing, and once I saw the necessity of reading I learned to do it well enough to make passing grades in college and seminary.

Today, I am still more of a listener and observer than a reader. I carry a lot of tapes with me in the car, and I talk with many people who can stimulate and inspire me. Most of my reading is concentrated in reference books, when I need specific information on a specific topic or question, and I use magazines to quickly absorb the gist of topics that would take much longer to cover in complete books.

The Difference Between Knowledge and Wisdom

Something that finally dawns on you as you enter adulthood is that skills and knowledge may be important, but as valuable as they are, they are not as useful as wisdom. Countless brilliant, highly trained, and highly educated people have become tragic failures because they lacked wisdom.

It's no accident that when given a choice of anything he wanted by the Lord, King Solomon didn't choose a Ph.D. in kingdom management or a master's degree in the economics of importing. Instead, he said to the Lord, "Give

*K*nowledge
is good,
wisdom is better.

your servant a discerning heart to govern your people and to distinguish between right and wrong."[3]

The Lord was pleased and told Solomon He would do as he had asked: "I will give you a wise and discerning heart," said the Lord, "so that there will never have been anyone like you, nor will there ever be."[4]

As a young man, Moses lacked the wisdom that God granted to Solomon. Not long after "graduating" from his education in Pharaoh's palace, he tried to break up a disagreement between an Egyptian and a member of his own Hebrew race. The Egyptian was abusing the Israelite and Moses, seeing that nobody was around, stepped in to take his countryman's side. In the ensuing fight, Moses killed the Egyptian and then buried his body in the sand.

The youthful Moses may have thought he had gotten away with something and done a "good deed" by saving a countryman from a horrible beating at the hands of a cruel Egyptian, but the next day he had to face reality. He came upon two Hebrews who were fighting and tried to break them up. One of them said, "Who made you our referee? Are you going to kill me the way you killed the Egyptian yesterday?"[5]

In no time at all, Pharaoh got wind of what Moses had done and put out an "all points bulletin" for his arrest. Moses didn't wait around and try to explain; he fled Egypt and wound up in the land of Midian.

So, in the first forty years of his life, Moses got what could be called his "start" in education. For the next forty years, his education would seem to come to a screeching halt. He married the daughter of a sheepherder and settled down to a life of total oblivion. Whatever Moses must have thought, his education continued during that second forty years of his life as he gained the patience, wisdom, and discernment he had needed so desperately when he was younger.

Just what is the difference between wisdom and knowledge? *Knowledge* is easier to define. When someone is "knowledgeable," he or she has mastery of a subject. Knowledge comes through accumulating a great many facts or principles and knowing how to connect one fact or principle with another. We often say, "He really knows his stuff!" or "She really knows her field, there's nobody better."

Wisdom, however, is harder to grasp. Scripture tells us, "Wisdom is supreme; therefore get wisdom."[6] Wisdom is like a precious jewel that is "more profitable than silver or gold and more precious than rubies."[7]

To me the jewel of wisdom has many facets, at least two of which are:

> . . . being able to use common sense.
> . . . being able to learn from your mistakes.

One of history's great examples of a man who learned from his mistakes was Thomas Edison, who is often called a "genius inventor." Edison, however, believed that "genius" was 1 percent inspiration and 99 percent perspiration.

One day two dejected assistants told Edison, "We've just completed our seven hundredth experiment and we still don't have an answer. We have failed."

Edison didn't agree. "We haven't failed," he said. "It's just now that we know more about this subject than anyone else alive. We're closer to finding the answer, because we know seven hundred things not to do. Let's not call these mistakes, let's call it an education."[8]

I also call it wisdom. We all make mistakes. It's not a question of avoiding mistakes; it's a question of what we learn from them, how we react and keep going toward our goals.

Sometimes all we need to do is apply a little common sense. Samuel Coleridge said that common sense, to an uncommon degree, is what the world calls wisdom.

The Janitor's Wisdom Solved the Problem

I love the following story, which beautifully shows how common sense can lead to a creative solution of a problem. Did you know that the glass elevator in the Tower of Hope on the Crystal Cathedral campus is inspired by the El Cortez Hotel in San Diego? The owners of that elegant hotel decided they needed additional elevators, so they hired a group of architects and engineers to figure out the best location, both in terms of appearance and cost.

As the reports came in, they discovered that putting additional elevators inside the hotel would mean cutting holes in all the floors. What a mess! Plaster, dust, and debris would be everywhere.

As the planners stood in the lobby deliberating over the placement of the elevators, a janitor overheard the conversation. He also was concerned about the mess the hotel was going to be in while all this reconstruction was going on inside. The more he thought about it, the braver he got, until finally he went up to the group of men and said, "Why don't you put the elevators *outside the building?*"

Everyone just stared at him for a minute. Nobody had thought of that. But the professionals listened and the idea clicked in their imaginations.

"Why not?" they said. "It's never been done before, but let's try to see how we could do it."

So the elevators were built outside the El Cortez Hotel, and since then many well-known buildings have used the same approach.

It took a common man with a commonsense idea to solve a big problem. That's wisdom!

I also like the definition of *wisdom* given by Denis Waitley. He says that wisdom is the ability to anticipate the probable effects of your decisions in other people's lives, as well as in your own life. Waitley believes that when a person honestly considers the well-being of others before he decides to profit himself, he becomes truly rich in the deepest sense.

In short, wisdom means living up to the potential God has put deep within, and that brings us to our third and final question:

Is My Education Drawing Me Closer to God?

The old saying tells us, "The more you learn the more you realize what you don't know." I have found that to be true practically every day of my life. The more I study and seek to grow, the more I realize how far I have to go. The larger I try to become, the more I am aware of how small I really am.

And the more I learn, the more I know I can't do it alone. There is so much knowledge, so much wisdom, so much taking place in this world, that it all points to a Supreme Creator and Sustainer of it all. There is no way the world could exist without God. The more I look into the things that are present and toward what is yet to come, the more assured I am that there is a God of love, a God of grace, a God of mercy, who loves us and wants to draw us closer to Him.

At the very core of wisdom is God Himself. Charles Spurgeon, one of the great preachers of all time, believed that wisdom is the right use of knowledge for God's glory. I can think of no finer model of this definition than Jim Poppen, who attended Hope Academy, a high-school division of my alma mater, Hope College.

Jim Poppen was not exactly an exemplary student. There were people at Hope Academy who questioned his intellectual capacity. Many of his teachers remarked, "I don't think he is ever going to amount to much. Jim Poppen just isn't very bright."

But Jim Poppen graduated from Hope Academy and

astounded his former teachers by going on to study at Northwestern University.

During one Christmas vacation, Jim's father awoke suddenly when he heard a noise in the night. Convinced that there was a burglar in the house, Mr. Poppen stole downstairs and tiptoed into the dark kitchen. There he found Jim tying knots around chair legs as fast as he could. Sure that his son had been studying too hard and had finally flipped, Mr. Poppen exclaimed, "Jim, what in the world are you doing?"

"It's okay, Dad," Jim explained. "I've decided I'm going to be a brain surgeon. I've got to teach my fingers to tie knots very fast and accurately where I cannot see anything—just like a surgeon operating in a human skull."

His father laughed and went back to bed. But Jim Poppen went on to graduate from college, attend medical school, and become one of the finest brain surgeons in the world.

When Senator Bobby Kennedy was shot in the head by Sirhan Sirhan, Jim Poppen was called in to try to save his life. When the son of Aristotle Onassis suffered critical brain damage in a plane crash, Jim Poppen performed surgery. In both cases, money was no object. They wanted the best in the world and Jim Poppen was the best.

But then Jim Poppen seemed to drop from sight. Friends finally tracked him down by telephone in a remote village twelve thousand feet high in the Andes in Bogotá, Colombia. They wanted to know what in the world he was doing there.

"Oh," he said quietly and matter of factly, "there are some people here who have some problems. They can't afford the high cost of medical care in Boston, so I decided to come here and take care of them."

For the rest of his life, Jim Poppen lived out his faith in Christ by serving people who were poor and in desperate need. When he died, the services held for him in the New England Memorial Baptist Chapel were jammed with great people whose famous faces many would know. But there were also many unknowns present: red, yellow, black, white, rich, and poor. Many nurses came to the chapel directly from operating rooms in nearby hospitals. They stood quietly in the back, still dressed in their green surgical robes and caps. Hundreds came to pay tribute to a man who was a living definition of wisdom—a man always ready to use his knowledge and skill at the right time and in the right place for God's glory.

Above all, seek and obtain wisdom. And whatever you seek for a tassel, it will be well worth the hassle!

Children Learn What They Live
(A Paraphrase)[9]

Children learn what they live, children live what they learn

If children live with criticism, they learn to condemn

If children live with tolerance, they learn to be patient

If children live with ridicule, they learn to be shy

If children live with encouragement, they learn confidence

If children live with security, they learn to have faith

If children live with fear, they grow up standing at the end of every line

If children live with praise, they learn to stand alone and lead their parade, even if it's raining

If children are spoiled with indulgence and permissiveness, they grow up full of compromise and greed

If children are given challenges and responsibilities, they grow up with values and goals

If children live with depression, they'll need a drink, a puff, a sniff, a shot, a pill to get them high

If children live with optimism, they'll grow up thinking they were born to fly

If children live with hate, they'll grow up blind to beauty and true love

If children live with love, they'll live to give their love away and become blind to hate

If children are reminded of all the bad in them we see

They'll become exactly what we hoped they'd never be

But if we tell our children "We're so proud to wear your name"

They'll learn to win, believing they'll achieve their highest aim

Because children learn what they live, and children live what they learn

6

Forecast Your Way to Fulfillment

"ROBERT, IT'S NOT like it used to be. Starting churches is a costly and time-consuming undertaking."

My father was speaking quietly in the dim light of the restaurant where we were having lunch. I had just told him that my brand-new position as Minister of Evangelism at the Crystal Cathedral didn't feel quite right, and that I thought the Lord was calling me to a preaching ministry in a church of my own, where I would be under pressure to prepare a sermon each week and develop my skills.

Dad didn't quite seem to hear what I was saying. He speculated that perhaps I could start preaching at the 8:00 A.M. service at the Crystal Cathedral, or perhaps the evening service?

"The Crystal Cathedral congregation is already developed, and it was drawn together by your ministry," I replied. "Preaching at one of its services wouldn't test my real ability to build a congregation. In my own church I could see if I have what it takes."

"Pray about it some more," my father advised. "There

are all kinds of opportunities to test your skills at the Crystal Cathedral. I think you should spend at least two or three years there."

We dropped the subject and spent the rest of lunch talking about ministry concerns at the Cathedral. But my mind didn't drop the idea at all. As Minister of Evangelism at the Crystal Cathedral—a job I had held only six months—I felt I wasn't challenged enough. I hadn't started with nothing, as Dad had done. My ministry had been generously handed to me. I had a plush office on the eleventh floor of the Tower of Hope, but where could I go from there?

I had it made, but I had made none of it myself. And where would I be in five years? Was it my destiny to stay in what was already feeling like a rut, and watch it slowly turning into a grave for my ambitions and dreams?

One of my father's favorite slogans flashed across my mind: "It takes guts to leave the ruts!"

Did I have the guts to move on? I left that lunch unsure, but I was still very restless.

Just a few days later I got the chance to see if I had only been talking or if God was really calling me out of safe, secure boredom to something different.

How About You, Robert?

I was in a church board meeting and my father had asked everyone to share what was happening in his or her life. Was there anything any of us wanted the others to pray about—any *decisions* we wanted help in considering?

What was Dad doing—setting me up to make an announcement? Then he turned directly to me and asked, "How about you, Robert? What is new and exciting in your life?"

I told the group about a new twenty-four-hour prayer ministry I was heading up at the Cathedral, and as I finished he asked, "Anything else?"

It was as if he were saying, "Share what's really on your mind, if you dare."

So I was being dared, or so it seemed to me. It was time to speak up or bite my tongue for another six months.

"I feel that God is leading me to start a new ministry—someplace, somewhere, sometime, somehow." (Was my voice as quavery as I thought it sounded?) "I don't know when, I don't know where, I don't know how." (My voice was definitely starting to break—I was losing it.) "I just know that God is leading me to start a new church."

Hot tears stung my eyes. "Excuse me," I managed, and left the room, thirteen shocked pairs of eyes following my every step. It took me several minutes to get a grip on my feelings, and when I returned to the meeting, the amazed look on Dad's face told me I may have read him wrong, that his question hadn't been a dare at all.

Everybody turned and waited for me to speak. "I want to be a great preacher," I tried to explain. "I don't believe I'll ever be able to be the man God wants me to be unless I stretch myself to grow. I've been praying a long time, and I really believe God wants me to get out and start my own church from scratch the way Dad did."

Tears welled up in my eyes again. Did I realize what I was saying? I was leaving the ministry of the Crystal Cathedral and all it involved. Everyone around that table grasped the implications.

The board members bombarded me with questions: What kind of ministry would I have? Where would I go? Would I start my own church? How would I gain the needed support?

"I'm just not sure of anything yet," I responded. "I don't know where God is leading me, but I want the continued guidance of His Holy Spirit and your approval. Will you give me that?"

All twelve members of the board stood with my father and me. We linked arms and everyone prayed for me. The meeting ended with lots of bear hugs, tears, and wishes of God's blessing.

I had taken the first of several important steps of faith toward a new chapter in my life. Since then I have realized that what was happening was really a four-step process:

Desiring a better destiny is that first and hardest step because it leads to making a decision. I had done that much, but my pilgrimage was just beginning.

Developing a strategy for success was a step that was still ahead of me. I had some rough ideas and plans, but that was all.

Doing what was planned was also still ahead, and I would quickly discover that the planning is easier than the doing!

Determining to persevere is what separates the "man of faith" from the "man of fade." I would almost fade several times in the next few years, but my training in my father's school of possibilities and persistence kept me going. In the months ahead, I would learn in a very special way that tough times never last, but tough people do.

Moses: The Reluctant Possibility Thinker

I call the four steps I outlined above a "forecast for fulfillment." I see them at work in the life of anyone who has ever accomplished anything, including Moses and the other giants we've been meeting in Faith's Hall of Fame.

In chapter 5 we looked at Moses' early life and saw how his education got him started and kept him going toward a unique relationship with God. Because Moses was such a giant on the biblical stage, we can study him in this chapter as well to see how he worked out his own forecast for fulfillment as he served God and his people.

I call Moses the "reluctant possibility thinker." We can pick up his story and find him on the backside of the Midian desert, far from Pharaoh and the bright lights of the Egyptian court. During his early years, he had received the best of educations from the Egyptians themselves, but he had never forgotten his roots. When Moses was a very small child his mother had drummed into him the tenets of the Hebrew faith, and he knew he could never desert his people or his God. Moses had desired a better destiny for himself and his people. But as we saw in chapter 5, all it got him was a prominent spot on Pharaoh's "Ten Most Wanted" list.

Moses had to flee from Pharaoh's wrath, and it seemed he was on the shelf. In fact, he spent forty years on that shelf, learning the patience and perseverance God would use later.

Moses might have lived and died on that Midian desert if God hadn't intervened. The Old Testament Book of Exodus tells us God spoke to Moses from a burning bush and told him to leave Midian, go back to Egypt, and free his people from Pharaoh's slave camps!

After forty years of herding sheep, you might think Moses would say, "Right on, Lord! I thought You'd never show up. I've been itching for action. Let me at 'em!"

Instead, Moses said, "Who? *Me?* Who am I to tell Pharaoh what to do? Besides, my own people won't believe You sent me—they'll laugh me out of town!"

It took a while for God to convince Moses he could still pursue that better destiny he had dreamed of forty years before. God had to show him he would have power to do signs and wonders and that he would have backup in the speech-making department from his silver-tongued brother, Aaron.[1]

Moses finally agreed to go, but I believe he was still quite leery about the whole thing. Going into Egypt to free the Israelites would be like going into Vietnam or Siberia to free the prisoners. And Moses was no Rambo; he was a fugitive who had settled down to raise sheep and a family on the back side of the desert.

You can get the rest of Moses' story from Exodus, as well as the eleventh chapter of Hebrews, where he is enshrined in Faith's Hall of Fame.

The biblical accounts tell us that *by faith* Moses:

. . . went back to Egypt and confronted Pharaoh with
an ultimatum: "Let my people go—or else!"

. . . backed up what he said when Pharaoh refused and
brought ten different plagues down on the Egyptian
countryside.

. . . saved the people of Israel by instructing them to
sprinkle blood on their doorposts on the night the
angel of death would pass over the land.

. . . led the Israelites out of Egypt and through (not
across) the Red Sea to freedom.

. . . continued to lead the Israelites through forty years
of wandering, fighting, starving, and dying in the
wilderness to finally bring them to the very edge
of the Promised Land.[2]

Because of their faith and their trust in God, Moses and
his people were able to find fulfillment in God's promises.
But they found that fulfillment only *through their faith*.
Their story is an epic example of how to live out a forecast
for fulfillment:

• Desire a better destiny.
• Develop a strategy for success.
• Direct your actions toward your plans.
• Determine to persevere.

Your Destiny Is Not Beyond Your Control!

I talk to many people who seem to believe *destiny* and
fate mean the same thing. If they are locked into a "going
nowhere" situation or job, they say, "I guess it's my
destiny, I guess it's fate."

There are at least two things wrong with that attitude:
First, I don't believe in "fate." If you believe God has a
plan for your life, fate is never in charge. Second, I don't
believe in letting my destiny shape my life. I prefer to
shape my destiny by moving out in a walk of faith.

Viktor Frankl, the Jewish psychiatrist who developed

the science of Logotherapy and who wrote *Man's Search for Meaning,* faced what looked like a horrible fate at the hands of the Nazis during World War II. He stood naked before the Gestapo. His watch had been taken, and then someone saw his gold wedding band and demanded that as well. As Frankl took the wedding band off his finger a thought flashed through his brain: *There is one thing you can never take from me, and that is my freedom to choose how I will react to whatever you do to me!*

As we saw in chapter 4, reacting to whatever life sends our way is a key to growth and a rung on the ladder to higher ground. I believe that at the moment Frankl handed over his wedding ring to his tormentors, he wasn't groveling in naked despair or just making brave talk in the face of a hopeless situation. He was daring to face what life had handed him and he was rising above it!

Obviously, when I chose to leave the Crystal Cathedral I wasn't in Frankl's predicament but the principle still applied. All my life I had dreamed of being a minister. I had said, "Daddy, when I grow up I want to be a minister, just like you." Because I had waltzed through high school, barely able to read and spell, I had to struggle through college and seminary. Now I realized that I still wasn't in the place God wanted me to be. Yes, I had grown up in one sense, but I still had some growing to do and I needed to get out on my own to do it.

While I knew I had to move on, I still felt ambivalent. True, it was exciting to think of starting something of my own from nothing. But it also had its scary side. My daughter, Angie, would be turning three in a few days, and another baby was on the way. Here I was, a young father, just out of seminary, with six months at the Crystal Cathedral to count as my "credentials of experience." I was leaving the security of a good position in one of the greatest ministries in the world to start something on my own, and only God knew where. Talk about Abraham daring to leave his people and his father's household![3]

"But you aren't in Abraham's league," the doubts whispered in my mind.

"Maybe not," my faith answered. "But I believe in the same God he did!"

As the pangs of second-guessing myself hit me full force, I ran my decision through my personal value system. A decision to step out into a new venture always prompts the questions of self-preservation. And so I had a little talk with myself in a mental dialogue that went something like this:

"Can I be sure of success?"
No, but if you think you can, God will!
"Is there a possibility of failure?"
Yes, but better to try something great and fail than attempt nothing and succeed.
"Is this idea risky?"
Yes, but only the one who risks is free.

Next, I went through some "service value" questions I had learned along the way. I had asked myself these questions before, but now they had new meaning.

"Will what I want to do help people who are hurting?"
Absolutely. In your own ministry you will be able to touch people with the widest range of hurts and problems.
"Will this make me into a better, more complete person?"
If this won't stretch you, nothing will.
"Will this bring out the best in me or the worst?"
You've been saying all along that you feel the unmistakable urging of the Holy Spirit to do this. God has a plan for you and it's a plan for good, not evil!
"Will this be a chance to prove my faith in a big God?"
You memorized the answer to that one a long time ago: You can do all things through Christ's power![4]

I have heard it said that, "decision making is easy if there are no contradictions in your value system." My value system checked out. I had desired a new destiny. I had made my decision. Now it was time to get up and get out!

Strategy Starts With Setting Goals

I have what I call a "magic" refrigerator. People laugh and tell me that's silly and I finally smile and say, "Well, actually you're right, there's nothing magic about my refrigerator, but it seems to work magic for me just the same."

"How?" they want to know.

And then I explain that when I decide to do or obtain something, I clip out a picture of that something or I make a simple poster with key words to remind me of what I want to do. I tape this picture or poster up on my refrigerator door where it is a frequent reminder.

I determine my destiny, I make a decision as to what I want to acquire, the position I want to gain, or whatever my goal might be, and up it goes on the front of something I wind up in front of many times a day. My refrigerator door becomes a billboard for my dreams and goals and helps keep me thinking about them all the time.

Thanks to my magic refrigerator, I can never elude my goals. I can't say, "Oh, I guess I really didn't want that," because there my goal is in black and white or living color to remind me of what I have committed myself to do. Sometimes reaching a goal gets tough. I start to ask myself, "Who needs all this stress and excitement?" My magic refrigerator always gives me my answer.

I decide I want a glass of milk or an apple and there are my goals saying, "Aren't we beautiful? We're waiting for you to do something about your destiny."

You see, first you have to desire a new destiny. Then you have to decide to follow through. When you post your goals where you can't miss them, you describe your destiny in a way that etches it into your mind. Your goals become part of you.

Do you want a promotion at work? Write your new title on a three-by-five card in big red or black letters, and tape it up on your refrigerator door.

Is the family car ready for the great parking lot in the sky? Clip out a picture of the kind of car you want and put it up where you can't miss it—on your refrigerator door. Then, when you are tempted to spend money on something else, you'll remember that that money has to go into the car fund.

On That Ranch I Will Build a Church!

When I grew restless in my work at the Crystal Cathedral, I desired a different destiny. I made my decision and announced I was leaving, but I had yet to *describe* what I really had in mind. It wasn't long in coming.

The day after I made my announcement, my father accompanied me on a drive to San Diego. I had a dental appointment; he just wanted time to talk with me.

As we rolled along Interstate 5, through the lovely Southern California coastland, Dad asked me how I hoped to buy property. I remember he said, "When I started my church, we were able to buy land for six thousand dollars an acre. Today it's more like sixty thousand dollars to six hundred thousand dollars an acre, and even then there isn't much vacant land to be had."

As we discussed financial realities, we passed the ninety-seven-acre estate of industrialist John Crean, the first man to donate one million dollars toward construction of the Crystal Cathedral. On a white stucco wall, the name RANCHO CAPISTRANO stood out in big, bold letters made of bricks, framed by hundreds of red bougainvillaea. At that moment I felt the Holy Spirit speak in an unmistakable way. What a spot to build a new church for God's glory!

I pointed at the RANCHO CAPISTRANO sign and said, "That's where I'm going to build my church." I did not say, " would *like* to build my church there," or "*Maybe* I could build my church there." I simply said, "That's where I'm going to build my church."[5]

"I believe it might be possible to get a gift of ten acres of that land for a church," I added.

Dad gazed out the car window as the lush hillsides of Rancho Capistrano sped by. I could tell he was getting enthused, maybe for the first time, over my new plans.

"Well, if you're willing to ask John Crean for ten acres of land, why not ask him for twenty?"

I caught Dad's enthusiasm and replied that if I were going to ask for twenty, why not forty?

By the time we got to San Diego, we had decided to ask John Crean for all ninety-seven acres! I would use part of it for a new church, and Dad would develop the rest as a retreat center that would minister to all kinds of needs, from emotionally depleted ministers to alcoholics.

It was on that drive to San Diego that my strategy started to jell. Now I had my goal clearly in mind. Setting a goal is an act of faith. It is describing what you hope will happen; it is the evidence that what you can't see is within reach.

At the heart of any strategy for success is the setting of goals that pull you toward victory. When the battle is joined, your goals have to be substantial ones—the kind that make you stretch and reach down deep inside to find more than you ever thought was there. I like Denis Waitley's observation:

> Goals we can reach with little or no effort have no pulling power; they're not the stuff from which winners are made. The excitement of reaching *toward* a challenging goal is often greater than the actual achievement. The joy is more in the reaching than in the grasping. Your goals must be demanding, requiring knowledge, effort, and performance to accomplish. With

an honest assessment of your talents and skills, you can set goals that are realistic, believable, and worth working for.[6]

I sometimes talk to people who have no particular goals. They tell me they are simply waiting for God to tell them what to do. I believe with all my heart in seeking God's leading. I know he led me out of the Crystal Cathedral and into my own ministry. I also believe that God puts desires into our hearts.

Some people believe it's not right to want a new house, a new car, or a certain piece of land to develop for a certain purpose, because it smacks of materialism or greed. Very often people reject ideas that come into their minds because they think God couldn't possibly have sent those ideas! It's as if they prefer to think God would send only grim demands to "be sure not to enjoy life too much!"

I believe that when we commit to a walk of faith, God leads us by putting ideas into our minds and then He expects us to set the goals to turn those ideas into reality. I like the words of Ari Kiev, a psychiatrist who taught at Cornell University. Dr. Kiev wrote an excellent little book entitled *A Strategy for Daily Living*, in which he said:

> Observing the lives of people who have mastered adversity, I have noted that they have established *goals* and sought with all their effort to achieve them. From the moment they decided to concentrate all their energies on a specific objective, they began to surmount the most difficult odds. . . . The establishment of a goal is the key to successful living.[7]

To that I can only add: The establishment of a goal is the key to any strategy for success!

It's What You Do That Counts

I sometimes ask my congregation, "If you knew you could not fail, what would you do?"

That's a powerful possibility-provoking idea! If you had put that question to me as I drove to John Crean's offices to ask him to donate Rancho Capistrano to the Schuller Ministries, I would have had no trouble answering it. I had desired a different destiny, and now my strategy for success focused on one major goal. What was I going to do? I was going to ask John Crean to catch my dream and provide the perfect location for a great new work for God in southern Orange County.

It was Maundy Thursday of Holy Week, just a day or two after I had announced my decision to leave the Crystal Cathedral. I realized it was five years to the day since my father had asked John Crean to donate one million dollars to make the Crystal Cathedral a reality. Was it time to ask him to donate his ten-million-dollar ranch to Schuller Ministries? It was rumored he was planning to donate the ranch to someone. Why not dare to live by faith and think that "someone" could be my father and me?

I parked in the lot of John Crean's forty-acre recreational-vehicle assembly plant in Riverside, California, and went inside to keep my appointment with a new destiny.

Acting on what I was sure was the leading of the Holy Spirit, I got right to the point. God was calling me to start a dynamic new church in San Juan Capistrano. Would John donate his ranch to make it possible?

At that moment my forecast for fulfillment ground to a sudden halt. John Crean responded to my request by saying that "only last night" he had deeded the entire property to the Jesuit Order of the Roman Catholic Church. It was his dream to have the ranch used as a spiritual retreat center and it was his opinion, from personal experience, that the Jesuits had more experience in running effective retreats than anyone else he knew of.

Small deeds done are better than great deeds planned.

It looked as if the case was closed. I had acted on what I believed was absolute, Spirit-led faith, and life had bounced back at me. I was getting a lesson in another truth that goes well with the act/react principle: "When God chooses to shut a door, get prepared. He's going to offer you even *more*."

I wasn't ready to give up. I reacted by asking John if he might carve at least ten acres out of the ranch that I could use for my church.

"No, Robert, I'm afraid that's impossible. The entire deal is set and it's out of my control. Why don't we go to lunch and we can talk about your plans a little more."

During lunch I started speculating about how I could raise enough money to buy ten acres of land in the San Juan Capistrano area. Property averaged nearly two hundred fifty thousand dollars an acre, and that meant a total of two and a half million dollars—an enormous amount of money for a small church to raise.

John chose not to join me in my possibility thinker's game. He caught me short by saying, "Start with nothing, Robert. Get out there and build a congregation. In fact, you might want to do what your dad did thirty years ago: start your church in a drive-in theatre. Why not the Mission Theatre in San Juan Capistrano? You could try working out an arrangement to hold services there."

I thanked John for his idea and said I would definitely think about it. On the way home I mulled over the entire conversation. I should have been able to read between the lines. Later, I learned that John felt I was a bit too young, immature, and inexperienced to take over something as big as Rancho Capistrano. Now that I look back I can see he was probably right.

In the next few weeks I began organizing Capistrano Community Church. One of my chief allies turned out to be John Crean's son, Johnny, who owned his own mobile-trailer plant in Chino, California. He agreed to be on my steering committee and expressed interest in joining the new church. Johnny and his wife, plus other key couples on the steering committee, held open houses and invited people who might be interested to hear my dreams for a new ministry in San Juan Capistrano.

I also contacted the Mission Drive-in Theatre, and with very little trouble negotiated a contract to use it on Sunday mornings. My forecast for fulfillment was in gear again! There had been a slight detour, but things were looking up. All I needed was a use permit from the San Juan Capistrano City Council.

When I appeared before them for what I thought would be a routine approval of my request, the ball came bouncing back into my court with stunning impact. The council turned me down. The reason? Holding church services in the drive-in theatre would cause a traffic jam in downtown San Juan Capistrano on Sunday mornings!

Door Number Two had slammed shut in my face. "Doing what you have planned" sounds simple enough when you list it as step three in a neat little forecast for fulfillment, but it was proving to be anything but easy.

What would Moses have done in my situation? To be honest, at that moment, in August of 1981, I wasn't thinking a great deal about Moses. But if I had, I would have seen that he had experienced any number of slammed doors and detours as he led the Israelites on a forty-year trek through the wilderness to the Promised Land. I was about to get some lessons in the same vital skill that brought him eventual success. I had always said I believed in perseverance; now I would get to practice it!

It All Comes Down to "Never Say Quit"

You may have heard the story about the overeager fan who approached the great Paderewski after he had given one of the greatest concerts of his brilliant career. "Oh, I'd give my life to be able to play as you do," said the admirer. Paderewski replied quietly, "I did."[8]

After getting turned down on using the drive-in theatre,

I began to suspect I might have to give my life to finding a place to start my new ministry. This business of taking God's dare to do something great for Him was getting a bit wearing. Acting and reacting was proving tiresome.

And it would get still worse before it got better. On September 4, 1981, John Crean called my father and invited my mother and him to drop over to hear some crucial news. The Jesuits had let the six-month option on Rancho Capistrano run out! The signed contract had never been returned and their time was up. John had decided to give the entire ninety-seven-acre ranch to the Robert Schuller Ministries and the "Hour of Power."

Significantly, however, my new church and I were not mentioned. As he discussed details with John Crean, my father said, voice shaking, "You know, John, this is an answer to prayer. It all started when my son, Robert, prayed for a place to start his new church."

John let Dad get no further: "Bob," he said with noticeable intensity, "I'm giving this to you . . . it is not for young Robert. He has to earn his own way. He has to experience his own struggles. It is my dream that this will be a retreat center, not just another church."

When I heard the news, I was a portrait in mixed emotions. Of course, I was happy for my father. He had achieved another victory in his long string of possibility-thinking triumphs. But I also felt the sting of John Crean's clear-cut rejection of my new ministry. Obviously, he felt I needed seasoning—to "experience my own struggles," as he put it. My father already had the Crystal Cathedral—I was out in the cold with no place to go, not even a drive-in. For the first time since trying to start my new ministry in the San Juan Capistrano area, I felt twinges of doubt. I sat down to have a talk with myself and the Lord. Was I acting in real faith or was I being presumptuous and cocky?

Spending an intense hour in prayer helped me conclude that I still felt ready to take on a new ministry and that God was calling me to do a great work for Him in the

Capistrano area. I also concluded that people in that area were ready to work with me to build this new church.

Despite the flat turndown on Rancho Capistrano, I was still absolutely sure the Holy Spirit had spoken to me about building a church on that beautiful piece of property—someday. Meanwhile, there was no alternative place to build, and I had to react by going in some other direction. Now even that other direction seemed to be closed.

I prayed, "Lord, I yield my work to You and put my trust in Your wisdom and perfect timing. When You say the time is right, I'll hear and act."

God Won't Lead if You Don't Want to Go

There is a story in Scripture about how the Prophet Elijah stepped out with tremendous faith and defeated four hundred prophets of Baal in a showdown on Mount Carmel. Yet the very next day he ran like a rabbit because he heard Queen Jezebel was upset with him.[9]

After what I thought was encouraging assurance from the Lord about what I was to do in San Juan Capistrano, I didn't run but I did drag my feet. In one sense, I stopped dead inside.

Oh, I made some halfhearted efforts to look at other locations—the Mission Viejo Mall, several grade schools and high schools, but nothing worked out, nothing was available or "seemed right."

I had the same problem Elijah had when he fled from Jezebel. I had lost my nerve. I was paralyzed by fear. It was the kind of fear I couldn't even admit to myself. From childhood I had been trained to consider fear as almost a dirty word. So when I started dragging my feet on starting the new church, I had all kinds of ways to disguise it.

I wanted to be sure I wasn't getting ahead of God. . . .

I wanted to be sure the Lord was leading me to His location. . . .

The truth was, my fears had caused the doubts to start

all over again. Maybe I had totally misread what God was telling me. Perhaps He had wanted me to stay at the Crystal Cathedral after all.

And so I began playing a game that fooled just about everyone—for a while. A week or two went by and then Johnny Crean called me and suggested we have breakfast. On the way to the restaurant I mused about how ironic it was that the son of the man who had turned me down twice on Rancho Capistrano had become one of my strongest supporters in starting my new work. Johnny had been trying to help me find a new location to hold our first worship services. Perhaps he had some additional ideas.

Johnny had something to tell me, all right, but he wasn't interested in playing my game any longer. Over a cup of steaming coffee, he said, "Robert, I know why you haven't found the place to start the church." The gleam in Johnny's eye told me he was on to something. What I didn't realize even then was that he was on to me!

"We just have to be patient," I told him. "God has the place and He'll lead us to it."

"He won't lead you if you don't want to go," said Johnny evenly. "The reason you haven't started the church isn't that you can't find a place. You and I both know you could start it tomorrow in any number of places. You could start it in your own backyard or living room, if you really wanted to. You're dragging your feet—why?"

Johnny had me. For the first time in several weeks I faced the fear I was afraid to admit was there.

"You're right. I am stalling. I guess I'm not sure God is really with me in this. Rancho Capistrano didn't work out. Then the drive-in fell through. I had always hoped for something different, unique, and special. Now I am afraid to make a move."

Johnny didn't judge or lecture. He just listened. Finally he said, "It's up to you. You can start the church if you want to. Maybe God isn't as concerned about the location as you are!"

I left that breakfast meeting with plenty to think about.

Johnny was right. I was dragging my feet. He and other interested people wouldn't wait around forever.

Franklin D. Roosevelt is known for a lot of famous quotes, including, "The only thing we have to fear is fear itself." He also said, "It is common sense to take a method and try it. If it fails, admit it frankly and try another. But above all, try something."

Do What You Fear—or Fear Is in Charge

Someone has said, "We must do what we fear or fear is in charge." I decided to quit stalling and try something—*really* try something.

One facility large enough to accommodate the church was Saddleback Community College, which I hadn't yet checked. I went to see the president, and he asked how he could help.

"I'm starting a new church and I need a place to hold services," I said. "Could we use the college gym on Sundays?"

"Why, yes," he said. "I don't see why not, as long as you agree to set up immediately before your services, put down the canvas tarp on the gym floor to prevent scuffing and scratching, and take everything out immediately after your service is concluded."

It all sounded like an incredible hassle at first. When I looked at the gym I discovered there was no heat in the winter and no air conditioning in the summer. It would have been easy enough to say one more time, "This doesn't seem quite right."

Then I remembered Johnny Crean's words: "You can start your church anytime you really want to."

"I'll take it," I told the president, and on November 1, 1981, Capistrano Community Church held its first services at Saddleback Community College.

I was learning to persevere, but I had barely scratched the surface. Over the next sixteen months, my "crew of the faithful,'' led by Nate Morrison, struggled with setting up equipment just before the services and then taking it down immediately afterward. During the winter months the congregation had to wear heavy coats while they sang hymns and listened to me preach. Through the summer months, a lone fan moved warm, humid air about the non-air-conditioned gym.

But we kept at it—every Sunday at 9:30 A.M. and every Friday night at 7:30 P.M. for what we called ''Family night service.''

I look back on those sixteen months as God's time of testing to see if I were really serious about doing a great work for His glory, not mine.

The beautiful location I had envisioned had not materialized. Neither had the huge crowds I had pictured coming to hear me preach. Oh, there were several hundred the first few Sundays who came out of curiosity to see what Robert Schuller's son was up to. And, of course, many of them wondered if I would show promise to match my father's charisma in the pulpit. But after three Sundays, my ''congregation'' dwindled to eighty-five people and hundreds of empty chairs. Here was the core of my new church. Very well, we would persevere together and see what God had in mind.

Capistrano Community Church grew steadily throughout 1982, but as we headed into 1983, I began to feel uneasy. We still didn't have funds to buy land and I wasn't sure how long we could keep using the Saddleback College gymnasium.

There is a place in the Book of Job where Job says, ''The thing that I have feared has come upon me.''[10] Sure enough, without a hint of warning, we received a notice that we had to be out of the gym by March 1, 1983.

I was beginning to get an inkling of what Job had gone through! ''We have no place to go,'' I told the college president. He replied, ''Sorry, Robert, the college board of trustees met and decided to no longer make the school property available to religious organizations on a continuing basis. I can't change their minds."

It was devastating news, but I vowed not to give up. All the clichés leaped into my mind:

> When the going gets tough, the tough get going.

> Winners never quit, and quitters never win.

I vowed I wouldn't quit and I did get going to find another temporary location. I tried everything, including asking many of the places that had turned us down sixteen months before. The answer was always no. And now I had too many people to shift services to my backyard or my living room.

I was out of options—except one. I went back to see John Crean. Would he change his mind and let us use the old warehouse on Rancho Capistrano for worship services?

John didn't say much, but he didn't give a flat no either. He would think about it that weekend when he and my father went deep-sea fishing together. Their agenda included catching a few marlin and discussing Dad's plans to develop Rancho Capistrano as a retreat center.

That was one long weekend! I don't know what I preached on Sunday, but I doubt it was patience.

Finally I got the long-awaited call from my father: "You've got the warehouse to develop on Rancho Capistrano," his voice boomed. "John is impressed with your work. You've proved yourself to him over the past year. You can start holding services on the ranch immediately."

I let out a whoop that I'm sure made Dad's ear ring for days. All the persistence had paid off. God had answered our prayers. We had reached our goal. Rancho Capistrano—"The Promised Land"—was ours. We were home at last!

Winning Isn't Everything After All

Vince Lombardi, the immortal coach of the Green Bay Packers during their dynasty years of the 1960s, is famous for supposedly coining this line: "Winning isn't everything; it's the *only thing!*"

I have learned, however, that those close to Lombardi who heard him speak many times, believe that what Lombardi really said was something quite different: "Winning isn't everything . . . but the *will to win* is everything!"[11]

You can desire a different destiny. You can develop your strategy around a worthy goal. You can do what you planned with decisiveness. But to reach fulfillment you must persevere.

In the end, your faith in God will give you the will to win. And *that* is what makes the difference!

Faith and Perseverance Are Invincible

Ray Kroc is famous for taking a promising restaurant operation located in San Bernardino, California, and developing it into the worldwide chain of McDonald's restaurants, where the number of hamburgers served has now reached what seems like infinite proportions. A favorite saying of Ray Kroc was also a favorite of Vince Lombardi:

> Press On: Nothing in the world can take the place of persistence. Talent will not; nothing is more common than unsuccessful individuals with talent. Genius will not; unrewarded genius is almost a proverb. Education will not; the world is full of educated derelicts. Persistence and determination alone are omnipotent.[12]

Combine Ray Kroc's philosophy with your walk of faith and you will have an invincible combination that God will use in your life far beyond whatever you have asked or thought.

7

Hope Against Hope When It's Hopeless!

AN OLD STORY begins as a man walked along the edge of the Grand Canyon. Somehow he missed his footing and toppled over.

As he plummeted toward the rocks hundreds of feet below, he flailed his arms, grasping at anything that might save him.

Somehow, his hand caught a small but tough bush growing out of a crack in the granite cliff. He hung there, hundreds of feet above the jagged rocks and the swirling river below. Then he looked up toward the edge of the cliff some fifty feet above him and could see no one. All he could see were the white clouds high above.

"Help! Is anybody up there?" he screamed.

A voice seemed to thunder out of the clouds, "I AM HERE."

"Who are you?" the desperate man shouted.

"I AM GOD!" the voice replied.

"Can you help me?" The man was desperate now. His arms were starting to go numb.

"HAVE FAITH," the heavenly voice commanded. "LET GO AND I WILL SAVE YOU."

The man glanced down again at the jagged rocks. Then he looked up once more and shouted, "Is anybody *else* up there?"

I've heard this story told many times, and it has become a favorite of mine. I know of more than one person who was converted while listening to this very story![1]

The joke has many applications. I especially like it because it illustrates the "Catch 22" we sometimes feel when we're trying to hold on to hope and someone says, "Let go and let God!"

Remember the beautiful definition of faith that Hebrews 11 gives us?

> Now faith is being sure of what we hope for and certain of what we do not see.[2]

That's a matchless definition. I have taught it to my own congregation. Life has taught it to me any number of times.

I notice, however, that we all need repeated lessons in what faith is all about. Faith may be "the assurance of things hoped for," but we can't always be so sure it's going to work out as we hope. Often we find ourselves dangling from the tiny shrub growing out of the cliff, holding on with one hand while we try to "let go and let God" with the other!

How can you hold on *and* let go at the same time? There have been times in my life when I have had to do just that!

Rancho Capistrano Started Like Camelot

In chapter 6 I may have left the impression that once we reached our goal of being able to locate our church at Rancho Capistrano, we went on to "live happily ever after." Do you remember the musical *Camelot?* It was in

Camelot that everything was going perfectly. Even the weather always cooperated, and rain never fell until after sundown. There was simply not a more congenial spot to live happily ever after in than Camelot.

But if you know the story, it didn't last. Eventually trouble filtered through *Camelot's* seemingly impregnable walls, and King Arthur and his knights faced all kinds of tragedy.

Our experience that first year at Rancho Capistrano reminds me somewhat of *Camelot.* When our church moved onto the property in March 1983, we renamed our congregation Rancho Capistrano Community Church. The old warehouse that we had been given to convert into a sanctuary and educational center wasn't ready to be occupied, so we met outside for the next six months.

It was one of the wettest springs in Southern California history, yet not once was our outdoor service rained out. It would rain to the north of us, it would rain to the south of us and the east of us, and the squalls would blow on the ocean to the west of us. But when we held services, it never rained on our Camelotlike setting.

Nate Morrison and his faithful crew would start setting everything up for the service at 8:00 A.M. each Sunday. I remember one Sunday morning when the situation looked rather hopeless. A call from Nate came to my office just as I was reviewing my morning message. It was exactly 8:00 A.M.

"What are we going to do, Pastor?" Nate asked. "We're here at the church, ready to set up the chairs for the nine-thirty service, but it's pouring cats and dogs."

I hesitated for a moment before answering, "But Nate, it isn't raining here and I'm just a few miles away."

"Well, you should see it down here! You'll be getting it soon."

"Wait and see if the rain lets up," I told him. "Set up by eight-thirty whether it's raining or not."

Nate was incredulous. "You mean we should set up in the rain?"

"That's right. We'll pray that God will stop the rain in time for the service."

I told Nate I would remain at the office until after 8:30, and I spent a lot of that time in prayer! At 8:45 Nate called back: "The rain stopped, Robert. Everything is ready for the nine-thirty service. I'm glad you told us to go ahead."

For the next fourteen Sundays, God continued to bless us on many days when it seemed hopeless. Rain would fall all around the district, but not one drop fell on Rancho Capistrano during services. The year 1983 was a year of record water damage in southern Orange County. Bridges and beaches were washed away and roads were destroyed, but we never missed a service.

In those early months at Rancho Capistrano, the ministry seemed to be going forward right on schedule. God was blessing us in many ways besides keeping the weather cooperative. We began a building program and soon had money raised for the remodeling of the warehouse into a church sanctuary.

The warehouse was a huge "Butler building" some two hundred feet long and fifty feet wide. It was constructed by erecting steel columns and then inserting prefabricated steel sections between the columns. The roof was also made of steel and the ceiling was sixteen feet off the floor.

Two sides of the warehouse had been redesigned with stone between the steel columns rather than the steel sections. John Crean had done this for aesthetic effects, to have a beautiful structure facing Interstate 5 as well as his own home up on the hill.

The other two sides of the building, which faced away from the freeway and the house, were made of the steel paneling. Every other section of the paneling was actually a huge sliding door. Mr. Crean used the building to house his collection of automobiles, which ranged from a dilapidated 1932 Ford roadster to a late model Lamborghini.

Except for the attractive walls on two sides of the building, all we really had was an empty shell, and we proceeded to raise three hundred thousand dollars to turn it into an attractive church facility with three major sections. At one end was the church sanctuary where a lovely stained glass window replaced one of the huge steel doors. At the other end were the Sunday-school rooms and church offices, and in the center was a large fellowship hall area that also doubled as our church foyer.

We are particularly pleased with the fellowship area because here people can congregate after a service and have plenty of room to stand around chatting, drinking coffee, and getting to know one another. They aren't pushed outside, nor do they have to go to some other area of the church for socializing. I feel this is a key to building friendliness and community in any congregation.

Big Trouble Comes to Our Camelot

That spring and summer of 1983 was a busy time as our membership increased to over two hundred and the bare shell of the warehouse began to turn into a sanctuary. As the busy days seemed to evaporate, I assumed my wife, Linda, was with me all the way in the new ministry.

I was wrong.

Actually, there were plenty of signs that pointed to trouble in our Camelot, but I was too involved in the new work to notice.

I should have been more aware that Linda's enthusiasm dampened noticeably when she saw that leaving the Crystal Cathedral and starting our own church hadn't gotten me very far away from my father. Because we were developing Rancho Capistrano together, I was still deeply involved with him. Linda would have preferred something very different.

And when invited to take part in planning the church functions or to join in a women's Bible study, she politely declined, saying that our new house and new baby took too much time.

After much searching we had finally found our dream

house in San Juan Capistrano, only three miles from the ranch. We moved there from our home in Irvine on July 1, 1983, just three weeks before Bobby, our second child was born.

But even more telltale signs started appearing early in the summer of 1983. One evening Linda and I were going out somewhere and I noticed she wasn't wearing her wedding ring. I mentioned it and she said, "Oh, I guess I forgot it."

But the ring turned up missing from her left hand on several other occasions, and when I confronted her she just laughed it off, saying she had forgotten it and not to worry about it.

I wasn't so sure. Linda had been seeing a psychologist for several months, complaining of depression. I had written it off to pregnancy blues and all the stress we were under with my leaving Crystal Cathedral and trying to get a ministry going in San Juan Capistrano.

In July 1983, her real problem came out and our Camelot started crumbling fast.

Hope Means Holding On

"Robert, I want a divorce," she told me one evening.

I tried not to take her seriously. She had talked about divorce several times during our rocky first year of marriage some nine years before. I tried to tell myself all that was behind us.

But Linda hadn't put it behind her at all. She brought it up again a few days later and I told her divorce was not an option. I would be happy to go to marriage counseling with her, but divorce was out of the question. I had been taught that marriage is for keeps and that you work out your problems, no matter what.

"Marriage is an institution," I told her. "Once you make a commitment to it, you stick it out. You hold on and make it work. I believe that's what we should do."

I felt twinges of irony as I made that speech. It was the same kind of advice I gave when I counseled premarital classes or when I talked to married couples who came to me to discuss their difficulties. Now I was holding on to my own marriage, praying that God would do something—and soon!

Linda continued to be unhappy, so I scheduled a session with a marriage counselor. During the first session we saw the counselor together and she asked Linda, "Do you want this marriage to work?"

I will never forget her answer: "No."

The counselor was not too encouraged, but she suggested that we use the "contract" approach to our problems. Each of us was to list items we felt were extremely important to building a good relationship, and then strive to satisfy each other's needs.

That's the way it went through the rest of the summer of 1983. I was hoping against hope that the contract agreement would help. But early in September Linda told me she had arranged to spend ten days with her cousin in the Midwest. She would be gone on the very Sunday we were to dedicate the new church sanctuary! Top leaders from our denomination, the Reformed Church in America, were going to be on hand to help dedicate the new building.

Heatedly, I told Linda, "If you aren't here when we have such an important celebration and I have to say that you're visiting your cousin in the Midwest, people will know something is really wrong with our marriage."

Linda shrugged. "Something *is* wrong, Robert. I'm going to see my cousin."

There was no doubt about it now. We had big trouble in Camelot. We were facing reality in San Juan Capistrano.

Faith Is Easy When Reports Are Good

As I opened this chapter I quoted the classic definition of faith from Hebrews 11:

Now faith is the assurance of things hoped for, the conviction of things not seen.[3]

That's an easy verse to quote when reports are good. I'm reminded of a deep-sea fishing trip I took not too long ago. Our boat was to leave about 11:00 P.M. We would spend the night on the water and then fish throughout the next day. On Thursday afternoon, several hours before casting off, we checked the fish report, which told us how many fish had been caught earlier. The report listed fifteen hundred albacore caught that very day! Albacore were what I was after!

A catch of fifteen hundred is a very promising fish report. It meant we were going to have a wonderful fishing trip. All of us—a group of about ten eager anglers—were so excited we almost needed anchors on our feet to keep from floating right off the boat. There was hope in that boat, because the reports were good!

When reports are good it's easy to have hope and faith. But what about when reports don't look so good? What kind of hope can you muster then? What do you do when you need hope the most, and the reports are bad?

During our tour of Faith's Hall of Fame in Hebrews 11, we have observed several giants of the faith:

- Abel had the right attitude.

- Enoch had the right walk.

- Abraham had the courage to take God's dare.

- Moses stuck to his game plan and persevered to bring the children of Israel out of bondage in Egypt and take them all the way to the borders of the Promised Land.

While all these men richly deserve to be enshrined in Faith's Hall of Fame, Abraham has a special place. Paul the Apostle immortalized Abraham as the man who was justified by faith and not by any works of the Law.[4] In fact, when Abraham lived, the Law had not yet been given. That was something for Moses to deliver to the people of Israel after God gave him the Ten Commandments on Mount Sinai.[5]

Abraham was known as "the man who believed God," and had righteousness or "perfection" attributed to his character.

Abraham received many discouraging reports as he made his pilgrimage of faith. Surely the reports weren't good when he said he was leaving the comforts of his home and moving somewhere out west. What about wild animals, bandits, bad weather, sandstorms? None of these reports stopped Abraham. His faith assured him of what he hoped for.

Later, Abraham received the most hard-to-believe report of all. God insisted that he and Sarah would have a child, even though both of them were well into their eighties. Abraham just laughed—it was better than crying.[6]

In "hope against all hope," Abraham still believed God and Isaac was born. In hope against all hope, Abraham became the father of many nations—even the father of Jesus Christ.[7]

When it looks as if there is no tomorrow, when it looks as if everything you've always dreamed for and hoped for is gone forever, what do you do? You hope against all hope! You believe in divine providence, the divine guidance of God, and you let faith step in.

To hope against hope is to reach for the stars, to dare to dream. There is a scene in Genesis where Abraham is brooding about the fact that he is growing old and he and Sarah have no child to inherit his estate. Abraham is afraid he will have to make a servant in his household his heir, but one night God speaks to him and says, "No, your heir will be a son who will come from your own body." And then God takes him outside and has him look up to the heavens and count the stars. God says, "So shall your offspring be."

And then the Scriptures say, "Abraham believed the

Lord and the Lord credited it to Abraham as righteousness."[8]

I believe that on that night God was telling Abraham to "reach for the stars and start a dream." Abraham was being dared to believe and to trust a big God—far bigger than he was.

Your Hope Is as Big as Your God

Have you ever stopped to think about how big God is? The Scriptures tell us that God created the heavens and the Earth. How big are the heavens and the Earth? It is two hundred forty thousand miles from the Earth to the moon, yet that's a mere fraction of the distance between Earth and Mars. Then think of the space between Mars and Pluto, which is millions of miles still farther out.

Even within our "tiny" solar system, our distances are almost beyond comprehension. And yet we are but one of many solar systems within the Milky Way. And the Milky Way is one of billions of other galaxies.

It is beyond the capacity of the human mind to understand how big, how vast, how glorious, how grand, and how beautiful God is. And yet from all His grandeur, magnificence, and size, God comes to touch the heart of any person who turns to Him in faith.

And with all of His splendor and grandeur, God is also a God of details. Scripture tells us He knows the number of hairs on our heads. He cares for the lilies of the field and for every sparrow, yet He cares for us much more than that.[9] God is interested in the details of your life. He knows exactly where you are at this moment and he knows every problem you face. He knows your frustrations. He knows when you are hoping against hope.

Dare to believe that God does love you. Believe it against all odds. Dream against all dreams that God does care about you and has a plan for your life and wants you to succeed. Look to God when the reports are bad, when there appears to be no hope. And as you hope against hope, God will hear your prayers. He'll hear your call and He'll come to you.

I love this verse in First Corinthians—it's one of my favorites:

> No temptation has come your way that is too hard for flesh and blood to bear. But God can be trusted not to allow you to suffer any temptation beyond your powers of endurance. He will see to it that every temptation has its way out, so that it will be possible for you to bear it.[10]

Hope Means Letting Go

I was desperately looking for a way out during that fall of 1983. The dedication Sunday for our new building came and went and Linda was not there. Many people asked about her and I simply said she had gone to visit her cousin.

The counselor and I met alone that week. I explained where Linda was and then asked, "What now?"

"Why not write to Linda and explain how you feel?" she suggested. "Tell her what you want out of your marriage."

I went home, sat down, and immediately wrote a five-page letter spelling out all of my hopes and dreams for Linda and me. I posted it that same day, overnight express. The next day Linda called.

"No way! There is no way I can possibly fulfill everything you want from me," she said shrilly. I tried to reason with her, but got nowhere. We had to hang up with nothing resolved.

Linda returned home about a week after that call and we went into cold-war status. I would be gone all day and after dinner, if I wasn't at a church function, she'd be gone.

Hoping against hope was getting rather hopeless. Our counselor, however, requested that we try to remain together until after the Christmas holidays. She wanted Linda to be absolutely sure she wanted the divorce and that ending our relationship was the right thing to do.

The last three months of 1983 were the most excruciating of my life. I couldn't share my burden with anyone. My mother and father had taught me that divorce is unthinkable, that marriage is for keeps. Their own marriage was a rock-solid example of that philosophy. I couldn't possibly go to them. And if I admitted our problems to anyone else, I was afraid any hope for reconciliation might be jeopardized.

For the first time in my life, I dreaded Christmas. It may have been the season of peace on earth, goodwill to men, but for me it signified the end of my marriage.

Linda did not relent. She remained cold and aloof through Christmas Eve and Christmas Day. I tried to play with the children, but broke down weeping. The pain became so great I left on Christmas night to stay at a friend's condominium for a few days. As I packed a bag, I thought to myself, *It's over—it really is over.*

When I returned a week later, nothing had changed. I had to learn that while hope is *H*olding *O*n *P*raying *E*xpectantly, there is a time when hope has to include letting go.

"We can't go on this way," I admitted to Linda. "Let's either get back together or let's file for divorce."

Her answer was immediate, no hesitation: "Let's file."

We went to see an attorney on Friday, January 6, 1984, and Linda instituted divorce proceedings. On the very next Sunday, I started a series of messages I had been planning for some time: "Getting Through the Going-Through Stage." They became the basis for a book in which I recorded the entire story of how our church started at Rancho Capistrano, how my marriage ended, and how God led me through the agony and trauma that followed.

As I closed my sermon on January 8, 1984, I told my congregation, "Two days ago my wife went to an attorney and filed for a divorce. Her decision was not made quickly or without counseling; still, it has been devastating for me. I know that we especially need God's love and your support to carry us through . . . please pray for us."

Somehow I got through the benediction, wondering, *Who are you to bless these people? Your marriage has failed. Where is hoping against hope now?*

The congregation stood to sing the first phrases of "In Christ There Is No East or West," their traditional response to the message. I sat down behind the pulpit and buried my face in my hands.

All hope seemed gone. I felt as if I were attending my own funeral. Would my ministry end right here?

As I sat there, head down, I heard footsteps coming across the floor, up the steps, and to my chair behind the pulpit. I raised my head and surrounding me were dozens of people!

There were hugs, there were tears, and above all, there were the words I so desperately needed to hear:

"We love you, Robert."

"We want to help."

"We're going to see you through this."

Hope sprang anew in my heart. It was as if God were saying, "Your ministry is *not* over. In fact, it might be just starting!"

As the star sends its laser of night-shattering light
Through billions of miles of hollow space,
So Lord, send Your love to greet me.
For I feel like eons have passed between
The warmth of Your tender touch
And me.

My marriage vows have been broken.
I have compromised my beliefs in the family.
My future looks bleak, barren, and lonely.

Please Lord, Shepherd me in the fruitful fields
Of grace, mercy, and peace.
Help me to believe in Your divine words.

Help me to comprehend Your undying, unending love for me.
Break through the caissons of my despair
And help me.

Robert Anthony Schuller
(written the week of the
divorce announcement)

Let Go—Nobody Else Is Up There!

This chapter opened with the story of the man who fell off the cliff, caught a branch, and screamed for help. A voice from above told him, "I am your God. I can help you if you let go."

The man replied, "Is there anybody else up there?"

It's an old story that's usually good for a laugh because we all identify with how that man felt. We face situations in which we aren't sure that the God up there can really help us, and we wonder if anybody else is available. That's foolish, of course. There is nobody else up there. Job knew that and that's why, when life had totally caved in on him, he could still say, "Though He slay me, I will hope in Him."[11]

There are times when life comes down so hard that "hoping against hope" seems foolish. During those moments you must hope the hardest. If it is true that when the going gets tough, the tough get going, it is even more true that when the going gets toughest, the tough hope harder than ever! Tough times never last, but tough people hope their way through.

Tara Nason, daughter of Mike Nason, producer of the "Hour of Power" television broadcast, was injured in a freak accident as a small child. She became paralyzed from the neck down and was condemned to spend the rest of her life in a wheelchair with a brace to hold her head up. There was "no hope" for Tara to live any kind of happy, normal life. Today Tara Nason is a teenager who paints pictures and types with her teeth. She writes beautiful poems and essays. She is living a happy, productive life from her wheelchair.

Joni Eareckson Tada is another whom the Lord seemed to "slay" for no reason. A careless dive into shallow water at the age of seventeen snapped Joni's spinal cord and condemned her to a life of quadriplegic hopelessness. Today, Joni has a ministry that has blessed and inspired millions of people.

Joni also paints and writes. She sings and speaks and testifies of her hope in the Lord. Her first two best-selling books, *Joni* and *A Step Further*,[12] told of her tragic accident and her struggles to find God's love in the midst of her pain and suffering. Her third book, *Choices . . . Changes*,[13] describes her far-reaching ministry, "Joni and Friends," and her marriage to Ken Tada, a high school teacher and coach.

Carol Schuller, one of my younger sisters, was in a motorcycle accident at the age of thirteen and lost her leg just above the knee. Her life hung by a slender thread as infection ravaged her body, but she finally recovered. Did she lose all hope? Her first words to me when I visited her in the hospital were these: "Bob, I know that God has great things in store for my life. I am going to be able to minister to people who normally wouldn't pay attention to me. God is using me for something great. He's preparing me for something special."

And Carol was right. After those first hopeless days following the accident, she learned to walk with a prosthesis. When she announced she was going to play softball, she was told playing a sport like that was "hopeless" but she did play and she scored her share of runs.

Then she announced she was going to learn to ski, another "hopeless" ambition. But Carol did learn to ski and has won gold medals competing with the International Handicapped Olympic Ski Team. Today she is happily married and expecting her first child.

Whenever I think of people who are inspiring examples of hoping against hope when it's hopeless, names like

*L*ord, as I hope against hope, give me the wisdom to know when to hold on when to let go and when to move out in faith.

Tara and *Joni* and *Carol* come to mind. They all suffered paralyzing and crippling trauma, and while I have never been physically injured as they were, I still feel we have something in common.

During those first weeks following the announcement of the divorce, I felt paralyzed. I thought my ministry had suffered a crippling blow. Storm clouds of guilt, depression, and despair gathered above me and I thought, indeed, it was hopeless. Then God gave me new hope. It came even in those first minutes after the announcement, when my congregation came forward to tell me they cared and they would be with me in this. More hope came when I went to talk with my father and we wept together. He encouraged me to hold on, and said that God would still use me in the ministry.

I did hold on. I did hope against hope and God did bring me through the valley of the shadow. The whole story is told in *Getting Through the Going-Through Stage*.[14] Today I continue my ministry at Rancho Capistrano with a new partner by my side. God reached out into my darkness and brought me Donna, who also knows something of hoping against hope when it's hopeless.

Hope Is Moving Out in Faith

We've talked about different facets of hope. There are times when you have to hold on, praying expectantly. There are other times when you have to let go and let God. And at the center of it all, you are hoping against hope, trusting God because He is the only One up there.

But hope is also moving out with the assurance that what you hope for is up there right ahead of you. There is a story about a salesman who lived in the 1800s and came from the East to a small frontier town in Texas. As he was dealing with a merchant in the local general store, a rancher came in to make a purchase.

"Excuse me," the merchant said, "but I have to wait on my customer."

Turning to the rancher, he said, "What can I do for you, Josh?" The rancher pointed to several items around the store, and then asked the storekeeper to put the bill on his account. "Oh," the storekeeper said knowingly, "so you want credit. Let me ask you something, Josh. Are you doing any fencing this spring?"

"Yes sir, I am," Josh answered.

"Well, are you fencing in or are you fencing out?"

"Going to add three hundred sixty new acres," was Josh's reply.

"Well, then, since you're fencing out, go ahead and see Harry in the back. He'll help you get whatever you need."

After Josh left, the Easterner said, "You know, I've heard of all kinds of systems of credit, but I've never heard of your system. What kind of credit is that?"

"Well," the merchant explained, "we've got two kinds of ranchers and farmers here: those who fence in and those who fence out. Those who fence in are people who are afraid they might not make it quite as well next year. They are afraid of what the weather might bring, or of wasting too much seed, so they pull their fences in. Then there are others who have confidence in themselves and their work. Slowly, gradually, they fence out, adding a little more land to their farms and ranches. People who fence out have hope. And I give credit to anyone who has hope!"

It is the same with God. As we hope against hope, even when it looks hopeless, we can fence out instead of fencing in. And He will give us unlimited credit in His bank of grace and blessing.

Let Go and Let God

As children bring their broken toys
  With tears for us to mend,
I brought my broken dreams to God,
  Because He was my Friend.

But then, instead of leaving Him
  In peace to work alone,
I hung around and tried to help
  With ways that were my own.

At last I snatched them back and cried,
  "How can You be so slow?"
"My child," He said, "What could I do?
  You never did let go."[15]

8

Give and Get Back Even More

WHEN JOHN CREAN donated all ninety-seven acres of Rancho Capistrano for development into a retreat center, as well as a home for our church, I was thankful and impressed: thankful because two new ministries could grow in such a beautiful setting; impressed because my search for church property had taught me something about the high cost of land in southern Orange County. John's ranch was appraised at well over five million dollars! But what I didn't know at the time was that the ranch represented fifty percent of his net worth!

The Gospel of Luke contains a principle of giving that I often share with my congregation. *The Living Bible* paraphrase of this text—Luke 6:38—says this:

> For if you give, you will get! Your gift will return to you in full and overflowing measure, pressed down, shaken together to make room for more, and running over. Whatever measure you use to give—large or small—will be used to measure what is given back to you.

When John Crean gave half of his net worth to God, the Lord gave back to him with full and overflowing measure! John is the major stockholder of Fleetwood Enterprises, a corporation with over one hundred factories throughout the United States. Fleetwood produces recreational vehicles, mobile homes, and prefab modular houses. When John gave away the ranch, Fleetwood stock was plodding along at five dollars per share and dropping, because gas shortages and high oil prices had cut severely into his RV sales.

At just about that time, the *Wall Street Journal* ran an article saying the wave of the future in housing would be prefabricated construction. And who did the *Wall Street Journal* name as a forerunner in prefab housing? Fleetwood Enterprises!

In the coming months, John's Fleetwood stock started to climb—from five dollars a share to ten dollars. Next it jumped to fifteen dollars and then twenty dollars. In a few months, it split at forty-five dollars per share. When it leveled off, it was selling at thirty-five dollars a share—fourteen times its original value.

For John Crean, Jesus' promise came true and then some:

> Your gift will return to you in full and overflowing measure, pressed down, shaken together to make room for more, and running over.

John Crean's story is a dramatic example of what happens when you give with no strings attached. Luke 6:38 is not a "quid pro quo" promise. God is not making a deal with you by saying, "I'll give you something if you give Me something." Luke 6:38 will not work if you try to strike a deal with God: "Okay, Lord, I'll give but I expect to be blessed—and please hurry, the income tax deadline is coming and I need some cash flow fast!"

Luke 6:38 works in your life when you give with no real thought of getting something specific in return. And it works in all areas of life, not just the financial one. It can be especially powerful in one-on-one relationships such as marriage or business partners. It does wonders in organizations or groups, especially a church. You can count on it: When you give with loving faith, you will get back far more than you give.

I've seen Luke 6:38 work in the lives of people in all kinds of situations as they become acquainted with the challenge of the word GIVE.

To give in faith means giving:

Generously
Intentionally
Visually
Eagerly

Faith Gives Generously

Giving is not really giving if there is no feeling of *generosity* involved. Giving money or property is one way to be generous. John Crean's ten-million-dollar gift of his ranch to the Lord's work was unquestionably generous. But there are other ways to be generous. For example, you can be generous with your time, the substance and stuff of your very life. All of us have the same amount of time, and the older we get the more precious it becomes.

The generous giving of time can bring an overflow return of love and affection that money cannot buy.

In 1921, Lewis Lawes became the warden at Sing Sing Prison. No prison was tougher than Sing Sing during that time. But when Warden Lawes retired twenty years later, that prison had become a humanitarian institution. It was a model for other prisons to follow. Those who studied the system said credit for the change belonged to Lewis Lawes. But when Warden Lawes was asked about the transformation, this is what he said: "I owe it all to my wonderful wife, Catherine, who is buried outside the prison walls."

Catherine Lawes was a young mother with three small

children when her husband became the warden at Sing Sing Prison. Everybody warned her from the beginning that she should never set foot inside the prison walls or in any other facility that the prisoners would be using, but that didn't stop Catherine! When the first prison basketball game was held, she insisted on going. She walked into the auditorium with her three beautiful children and sat in the stands with the hard-core criminals. Other guests came to her afterward and asked, "How did you dare sit with those men? Why did you take you little children in there?"

And her reply was, "My husband and I are going to take care of these men, and I believe they will take care of me! I don't have to worry!"

She even insisted on getting acquainted with the records of the men. She discovered that one of the men convicted of murder was blind, so she paid him a visit. She stepped into the cold cell and sat down next to this man. Holding his hand in hers she warmly said, "Do you read braille?"

"What's braille?" he asked.

"Don't you know? It is a way that you can read with your fingers," she explained.

"Well, I've never heard of it," he replied.

"Then I'll teach you!" she enthused. And she taught that blind killer how to read braille. Years later he would weep in love for her.

Later Catherine found that there was a deaf-mute in the prison, so she went to school to learn sign language. Soon she was communicating with him through the use of her hands. Many said that Catherine Lawes was the body of Jesus Christ that came alive again at Sing Sing Prison from 1921 to 1937.

Then one evening the car in which Catherine was riding went out of control, and she was killed. The next morning her husband did not come to work; the acting warden came in his place. In an instant, the whole prison knew something was wrong. When they heard the news that their beloved lady had died, everyone wept.

The following day Catherine's body was resting in a

casket in her home, three-quarters of a mile from the prison. As the acting warden took his early-morning walk, he was shocked to see a large crowd of the toughest, hardest-looking criminals gathering like a herd of animals at the main gate. It looked as if they were ready to launch a riot. He walked over to the group, and instead of seeing hostility in their eyes, he saw tears of grief. He knew how much they loved and admired Catherine.

He turned and faced the men. "All right, men, you can go. Just be sure and check in tonight!" Then he opened the gate without another word, and a parade of more than one hundred criminals walked, without a guard, three-quarters of a mile to stand in line to pay their respect to Catherine Lawes. And every one of them checked back in that night![1]

Catherine Lawes was never rich by monetary standards, but she was rich beyond imagining in the love and goodwill those convicts returned in full and overflowing measure, pressed down, shaken together to make room for more, and running over.

It takes courage to give as Catherine Lawes did, but she gave generously of all she had, and the returns were beyond counting.

Scripture's pages are filled with people who gave of themselves and were blessed to overflowing in return. We've already seen the overflowing principle at work in Hebrews 11. We see it blessing Noah, who poured his life into building the ark (scholars believe it took at least one hundred years), and who was blessed by becoming the man through whom the human race got another chance.

Abraham was ready to give Isaac and God stayed his hand and gave back to him a heritage that blessed the entire earth.

Another generous giver who is listed in Faith's Hall of Fame in Hebrews is Rahab. At first glance, a harlot is an unlikely choice for any kind of Hall of Fame, but Rahab is named along with the other blue bloods *because of her faith*. When the Hebrew spies needed shelter during their mission to learn the strength of Jericho, Rahab gave them hospitality at the risk of her life. Later, they in turn spared her family and her when they returned with the Israelite army to besiege.[2]

Faith Gives Intentionally

In order for something to be a true gift, it has to be given *intentionally,* not grudgingly, or by accident.

If I lose something and my wife finds it, that's not my gift to her. For it to be a gift, I must present it to her face-to-face, or at least with a card that says, "From Robert, with love."

When I conduct a wedding ceremony, I explain to the bride and bridegroom that a giving relationship is not a 50/50 proposition. In a 50/50 break-even relationship, no intentional giving takes place. There are trade-offs and deals, to be sure, but no real gifts are exchanged. Only in the 51/49 relationship does giving start to occur in even the smallest way. In the 55/45 relationship, even more giving is going on, and obviously 60/40 is better yet.

I advise newly married couples to shoot for a 60/40 marriage or better. I stress that I don't mean, "She gives sixty and you give forty," or vice versa. I mean that both parties should seek to give 60 percent, or even more, to the marriage. Then and only then is there giving that is intentional, done out of a generous heart that seeks more for the other than for itself.

Where Had Camelot Gone Sour?

During those last months of 1983 and the first months of 1984, I kept wondering what had happened. Where had Camelot gone sour? Had Linda and I had a 60/40 marriage? Apparently not.

It was during this time, when I desperately needed a

friend, that God introduced me to Donna. We met for the first time, December 26, 1983, on a misty, overcast beach near the condominium where I was staying. The pain of that last Christmas with Linda and the children was so great I had to get away, and I went to stay with a friend in Laguna Beach.

My spirits were more overcast than the sky, and I decided to go for a walk in what was practically a light rain. I came around a large rock protruding out of the sand, and there was a tall, lovely blonde—the only other person on the entire beach. We said hello and struck up a polite conversation.

I learned that her name was Donna. I gave her my name, and almost immediately I blurted out that I was married and had two children. I could see she was curious. If I had a family, why wasn't I with them the day after Christmas? I explained that Linda and I had separated and she was planning to file for a divorce in a few days.

It turned out Donna was going through a very similar trial. She had been separated from her husband for a year and a half and he also was planning to file for a divorce. We walked along the beach together and talked and agreed to meet again and talk some more, if possible. She seemed to offer me friendship, a listening ear, someone in whom I could confide.

In the next few weeks, I met Donna several times for coffee and we continued to share our problems. She became my counselor and my friend.

As our relationship progressed, our friendship blossomed into romance. I'm not sure why Donna kept seeing me during those first few weeks and months. Later she told me quite candidly, "I don't know why I put up with you. It must have been the Lord bringing us together. If it had been up to me, I wouldn't have continued to see you. I had enough problems going on in my life already."

But Donna was patient. She listened as I wrestled with everything from my guilt and doubts about deserving to be a minister any longer to my anger and lack of forgiveness.

As the weeks and months of 1984 sped by, Donna and I found we had more and more to share. We particularly liked exchanging favorite books. Among them was *The Road Less Traveled,* Scott Peck's brilliant assessment of love, values, and spiritual growth.

I especially liked Peck's opening line: "Life is difficult." Much of what Peck had to say gave me new insights into what a 60/40 marriage could be. At one point he wrote:

> When I genuinely love, I am extending myself, and when I am extending myself, I am growing. The more I love, the longer I love, the larger I become. Genuine love is self-replenishing. The more I nurture the spiritual growth of others, the more my own spiritual growth is nurtured.[3]

By the fall of that year, Donna and I had committed ourselves to marriage, a marriage based on intentional 60/40 giving. In fact, we try to go better than 60/40 as we build our family: Angie, nine, Bobby, six, and Christina, our one-year-old daughter.

Faith Gives With Vision

Giving in faith means you can *visualize* God's blessing. "Faith is the evidence that what you can't yet see will mature and bear fruit. Faith is the assurance of things hoped for, the evidence of things not seen."[4]

When you give, it is an act of hope—of faith. You expect a return.

When a farmer plants his seed, he hopes for a crop—100-fold if God so chooses to bless.

Remember, you don't *demand* a return from God, but you can *expect* it in faith. When you give by faith, you visualize God at work. You have a hope, a dream. You know that what you give will be given back. You don't

*W*hen you give, you can't demand a return from God, but you can expect it.

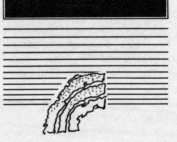

know exactly how or when, but you can see God's blessing coming into your life—pressed down, shaken together, and running over.

I like the way Oral Roberts opens his television program: "Something *good* is going to happen to you." The giver who understands the secret of fruitfulness believes something good is going to happen. The seed you plant in the form of money, time, caring, or serving will indeed grow and produce the fruit of joy, patience, prosperity, peace—union with God Himself.

Giving visually is inseparably linked to giving generously and intentionally. When you give generously and intentionally, you can expect a return. You have God's word on it in Luke 6:38.

The Difference Between Heaven and Hell

There is a story of a man who had a dream one night. He dreamed that he died and found himself in a large room. In the room there was a huge banquet table filled with all sorts of delicious foods. Around the banquet table were people seated on chairs. They were obviously hungry. But the chairs were five feet from the edge of the table and the people apparently could not get out of the chairs. Furthermore, their arms were not long enough to reach the food on the table.

In the dream there was a solitary large spoon, five feet long. Everyone was fighting, quarreling, and pushing, trying to grab hold of the spoon. One man reached out, picked up some food, and turned it to feed himself, only to find that the spoon was so long that as he held it out he could not touch his mouth. The food fell off.

Immediately, someone else grabbed the spoon. That person reached far enough to pick up the food, but could not feed himself. The handle was too long.

In his dream, the man who was observing it all said to

his guide, "This is hell; to have food and not be able to eat it."

The guide replied, "Where do you think you are? This *is* hell. But this is not your place. Come with me."

They went into another room. In this room there also was a long table, filled with food, exactly as in the other room. Everyone was seated in chairs, and for some reason they, too, seemed unable to get out of their chairs.

Like the others, they were unable to reach the food on the table. Yet they had satisfied looks on their faces. Only then did the visitor see the reason. For exactly as before, there was only one spoon. It, too, had a handle five feet long. Yet no one was fighting for it. In fact, one man who held the handle reached out, picked up food, and put it into the mouth of someone else, who ate and was satisfied.

That person then took the spoon by the handle, reached for the food from the table, and put it back to the mouth of the man who first gave him something to eat. And the guide said, "This is heaven."[5]

I believe heaven will be filled with those who have experienced the greatest gift of all, salvation in Christ, and who have given generously and intentionally to bring happiness to others without concern for their own. When you give out of faith, you don't look for a blessing, but you never fail to see it materialize in your life.

Faith Gives Cheerfully and Eagerly

The Scriptures tell us God loves a cheerful giver.[6] I can think of no better story of eager, cheerful giving than the one that starts with my grandmother's apple pies.

Grandma was a beautiful woman in many ways, and one of the generous things she did for her grandchildren was to bake delicious apple pies for them.

When I was young I would spend almost every summer at Grandma's farm in Iowa. Often she would give me a bucket and say, "All right, Bobby, go gather the apples and I'll make you a pie."

So I'd go out to the orchard of old crab apple trees and gather up all the apples that had fallen to the ground. I'd haul them into the kitchen and Grandma would sit down to peel and slice them. Then she'd roll out the dough, mix the apples with cinnamon and sugar, put the pies together, and pop them into the oven. The aroma of those baking pies was unbelievable! When they came out of the oven they looked six inches high. And the taste! The taste wasn't unbelievable. It was incredible!

Hands down, my grandma made the best apple pie in the world.

Grandma died in 1972. In 1983 the Hour of Power Ministries received through the mail a check for $68,400, the largest unsolicited gift ever given to the ministry up to that time. There had been no special appeals, but suddenly, for no apparent reason, this huge check arrived with the rest of the day's mail.

My father saw the check, and noting the rather shaky handwriting, he guessed it had been sent by an elderly person. The address on the check was Sioux Falls, Iowa, which is thirty-five or forty miles from the Alton area where my father had been raised on Grandma's farm.

Dad was curious, so using the phone number printed on the check, he called the lady to say thank you.

When he got her on the phone, Dad said, "Hello, ma'am, this is Robert Schuller. You sent us this wonderful donation. I just wanted to thank you for it."

She said, "Oh, you're very welcome."

"Tell me about yourself," my father went on. "What did you used to do? The note with your check says you're retired now."

She said, "Oh, yes, I used to be a schoolteacher. I taught in many different towns in northwest Iowa."

"By any chance, did you ever go to Alton?" my father inquired.

"Why, yes. In fact, I was born in Alton and later I taught elementary school there."

My father began to get excited as he asked, "By any chance did you know my mother? Her name was Jenny Schuller."

The lady replied, "Why, as a matter of fact, I did know Jenny Schuller and I'm well aware she was your mother. She brought my sister an apple pie when she was sick. I realized that if she was that nice and that kind to somebody she hardly knew, then your ministry must be honorable and reputable, the kind of organization I'd want to give to. I have a little house and it's paid for. It requires very little upkeep anymore and I had the savings I collected through the years. I didn't know what to do with the money, so I just decided to give it to your ministry."

And so an apple pie, baked and given with love by my grandmother, planted a seed of goodwill and gratitude that produced the largest unsolicited gift the "Hour of Power" had ever received.

My father is fond of saying, "Any fool can count the seeds in an apple, but only God can count the apples in a seed." That's true, and only God can count the blessings that come from the gift that is given eagerly by the cheerful, generous giver!

Give to Produce Hope, Love, and Life

The secret of fruitfulness is to give generously and intentionally, visualizing God's blessing as you eagerly share what you have with Him and others. As you give, you will get. Your gift comes back to you in greater measure than you ever gave, when you give in faith. Giving out of faith produces hope, love—and life.

No one knows this better than Benno Fischer, an architect whom I met ten years ago while he was working on the Garden Grove Community Church. I noticed a *KL* tattooed on his hand and I asked, "What does *KL* mean?"

He told me, "That means *koncentration larga*—concentration camp." And then Benno told me the story of how he had survived the *KL:*

> The Nazis rounded us up like cattle and threw us all into the concentration camp. We started with four thousand men, and by the time we were freed only four hundred were left.
>
> The Nazis rationed the food and gave each man a cup of soup and a cube of bread each day. The soup was thin, but at least it was hot and fairly tasty. Men would come and beg me to trade my soup for their bread, which was dark, tough, and often dry. They were desperate and so, while I didn't like the bread much better than anyone else did, I would trade away my soup to help bolster their spirits and keep some spark of hope alive.
>
> What I didn't realize was that, while the soup was hot and tasted good, there was less nutrition in the soup than in the bread. I watched man after man die of malnutrition, and almost always it was someone who preferred soup to bread. Only four hundred of us survived. We were the ones who were willing to give our soup for bread.

People everywhere seek to learn the secret of a happy, fruitful life. The secret is to give instead of desiring to get. First give your life to Jesus. Then give what you can—a song if you sing, a loaf of bread if you bake, a dollar if you have the means. Above all, use the 60/40 principle in all your relationships, especially your family.

> For if you give, you will get! Your gift will return to you in full and overflowing measure, pressed down, shaken together to make room for more, and running over![7]

How to Give When You Disagree

In *The Positive Family*, my mother, Arvella Schuller, shares her secret for how she and my father could be married successfully for over thirty years, even though they don't always agree. She explains that they have a scale of nonapproval. When she and Dad disagree, they measure the depth of the intensity of nonagreement on a scale of one to ten:

1. The lowest level is, "I'm not enthusiastic, but go ahead if you want to." From there the intensity of the comments increases.
2. "I don't see it the way you do, but I may be wrong, so go ahead."
3. "I don't agree. I'm sure you're wrong. But I can live with it. Go ahead."
4. "I don't agree, but I'll be quiet and let you have your way. I can change it to my way later on. Next year I can repaint, repaper, reupholster it my way."
5. "I don't agree, and I cannot remain silent. I love you, but I will not be able to keep from expressing my disapproval. So don't be offended if you hear me expressing a contrary view."
6. "I do not approve, and I make a motion we postpone and delay action until we both are able emotionally and rationally to reevaluate our positions. Give me more time."
7. "I strongly disapprove. This is a mistake—costly, not easily corrected—and I stand firm. I cannot and will not go along with it."
8. "My answer is no! I will be so seriously upset if you go ahead that I cannot predict what my reaction will be."
9. "No way! If you go ahead I have to tell you I quit; I'll walk out!"
10. "No—no—no! Over my dead body!"[8]

My father maintains that in more than thirty years of marriage he and Mom never went above a six in their level of disagreement. As I think back to growing up in their home, I would say that he is correct, for the most part. They may have hit a seven or an eight once or twice, but they usually stopped at number six, which really means, "I love you very, very much. Since I can't tell what this is going to do to our relationship, which is obviously more important than the decision, let's wait and think about it . . . give me time to see your viewpoint and feel what you feel."[9]

That's the attitude of a 60/40 marriage. That's the attitude Donna and I try to maintain daily.

9

---

*Take the Faith
and
Run the Race!*

I GOT THE phone call in late July, the day before the opening of the 1984 Olympic Games in the Los Angeles Coliseum. It was my sister, Carol, calling from Hawaii.

"Bob," she bubbled. "You can't guess what I have."

"What's that?"

"A spare ticket to the opening ceremonies to the Olympics tomorrow! Would you like to go with me? I'm flying in tonight."

"You only have one, huh?"

"Yep, only one, besides mine. You and I can go together."

"Well, this is a problem. I really want to go, but I've already got a commitment. I promised to take Tom Tipton fishing tomorrow. Only thing is, my boat is in the shop and it's supposed to be ready this afternoon. If it's ready, I have to say no because of my commitment to Tom."

"Can you find out and let me know?" Carol asked. "I can try to get someone else to go."

"I'll get right back to you—count on it!" I said as I hung up.

I called the boat shop and heard "bad news" that was really good news.

"Sorry, Mr. Schuller, we can't have your boat ready 'til Monday."

"Thank You, Lord," I said to myself, and then said aloud to the repairman. "No problem. I'll pick it up on Monday."

Next I called Tom, took a rain check on the fishing trip, and rescheduled it for the following Friday. Then I called Carol back and said, "I can go! By the way, how much is it going to cost?" (I didn't want to commit to something and then find out the price was a thousand dollars.)

"Nothing, Bob, it's free."

"Wow! Everything's looking pretty good here," I said. "See you tomorrow!"

We hung up, and I walked around on air all day. Things looked very good. I was going to spend the day with my sister, Carol, which I always enjoyed. And, we would see a once-in-a-lifetime event to boot!

Furthermore, the Olympics were in the right place—Los Angeles. I didn't have to fly to Moscow or Seoul to take advantage of the offer.

And the price was certainly right. I can't think of a better deal than "free."

And so Carol and I did go to the opening ceremonies of the 1984 Olympic Games. We saw all the fanfare and it was a spectacular, wonderful day I'll never forget. That call from Carol was an invitation I could not refuse—and I'll always be glad I didn't.

Why Refuse a Fantastic Invitation?

Have you ever gotten an invitation you couldn't refuse? How about the invitations you did refuse, even though they sounded fabulous? What is it that causes us to turn down beautiful opportunities, fantastic invitations? I think it's usually one or more of the following:

Wrong people.
Wrong place.
Wrong price.
Wrong prize.

On this final leg of our tour of the life of faith, we come to an invitation we can't refuse. It has the right people, the right place, the right price, and the right prize. In fact, it's the greatest prize of all: the prize of joy, peace, prosperity. The prize is fullness and wholeness of life. The prize is wellness of soul, body, and mind. The prize is *all* these things wrapped in the salvation that comes through Jesus Christ.

Why do some people refuse a prize like this? I often ask myself that question, and I believe it's because they get the wrong idea or wrong information about the people, the place, and the price that go along with this greatest prize of all. They reject Jesus because they have a wrong perspective, a wrong attitude. They refuse the greatest invitation ever given to mankind because they don't bother to check it out and get all the information they need to make a decision.

Our look at the life of faith has centered in the eleventh chapter of Hebrews, which opens with a definition of *faith* we should now know by heart:

> Now faith is being sure of what we hoped for and certain of what we do not see.

We have seen what Abel, Enoch, Noah, Abraham, Moses, and Rahab all accomplished—*by faith*. And then the writer of Hebrews says he doesn't have time to tell us about Gideon, Barak, Samson, Jephthah, David, Samuel, and the prophets.[1] Because these people all trusted God, they won battles, overthrew kingdoms, ruled well, and received what God had promised.[2]

And there are still more, a host of unnamed others who escaped death by sword or sickness, who were given great power in battle, who got loved ones back from death. And still others who trusted God and were beaten to death, laughed at, whipped until their backs were raw, stoned to death, sawed in two, and forced to wander hungry, sick, and ill-treated, hiding in dens and caves.[3]

Then Hebrews tells us a curious fact: All these people trusted God and won His approval through faith, *but not one of them received everything that God had promised.* Why? Because God had a better offer that He planned to give later—a better prize that He wanted all of them to share with all of us who live today.

That better way is Jesus Christ; He is the invitation we can't refuse.[4]

Today's Bibles include some features that weren't in the early editions or the original manuscripts. I'm talking about chapter headings and verses that were added later by scholars strictly for reference purposes. To get a beautiful description of the invitation we can't refuse, we must go on to Hebrews 12:1, 2:

> Therefore, since we are surrounded by such a great cloud of witnesses, let us throw off everything that hinders and the sin that so easily entangles, and let us run with perseverance the race marked out for us. Let us fix our eyes on Jesus, the author and perfecter of our faith, who for the joy set before him endured the cross, scorning its shame, and sat down at the right hand of the throne of God.[5]

All that great cloud of witnesses—all those people mentioned back in Hebrews 11—are watching. We are being invited to strip off everything that slows us down and holds us back. We want to put away all of our excuses, everything that keeps us from taking that leap of faith and running the race set before us.

These first two verses in Hebrews 12 invite us to become spiritual Olympians—to run the race of life with Jesus Christ to gain a prize that is beyond price. There is no good reason to refuse this invitation. The price is right, the place is right, and the people are right. Let's look at all of them to see why.

You Run With the Right People

Suppose someone called you and said, "Hey, I have a spare ticket for the opening ceremony to the Olympics—want to go?" You would probably accept, but then what if the caller added, "Oh, yes, the section where you'll be sitting includes people who are under surveillance for possible terrorist activity. Don't worry, though, there will be plenty of guards around and they can probably stop them before they blow anybody up."

The people you're with do make a difference. If I couldn't trust the people sitting around me, I doubt I would accept a free ticket—to the Olympics or to anything else.

What about the people surrounding you when you decide to take the faith and run the race with Christ? I believe this invitation is for two kinds of people: veterans and new recruits.

The veterans are those who have already accepted Christ's invitation to join Him in the race. In fact, many of them have been racing for quite a while, and frankly, they may be a bit tired. These verses in Hebrews are urging the veterans to strip off some of the cynicism and doubts that have accumulated along the way. Perhaps there are some sins that keep their feet tangled up. There may be negative thinking and actions that are tearing them and others down. Whatever it is, the people who believe they're already in the race and walking in faith with Christ are invited to get in shape and run a better race than ever.

But this invitation is also meant for people who haven't quite made up their minds. They may be hanging around the outside of the stadium, so to speak, wondering if joining this particular Olympic team is worth it. They are being invited to become new recruits. Through placing their faith in Jesus Christ they can strip off all the feelings of inferiority, lack of confidence, poor self-esteem, guilt, frustration, and fear. They can commit to running a race with excellence and be surrounded by people who are trying to do the same and who will help them along their way.

What About All Those "Hypocrites"?

"Wait a minute, Robert," you might be saying. "What about all the hypocrites in this race? What about all the phonies who are in churches who say they worship Jesus Christ?"

I often get asked the question "What do you do?" It's a common question we ask one another when we meet for the first time. When I meet someone, I try to get acquainted by asking about his family, his occupation, his favorite recreation, and so on. People often ask the same questions of me.

I always get an interesting reaction when somene says, "Well, what do you do?" and I reply, "I'm a minister."

More often than not the conversation becomes stiff or cool in a hurry. I don't know why ministers make people nervous, but for some reason they do.

So, I often sidestep that question by saying, "I'm a speaker," or "I'm in administrative work." A minister has all kinds of duties, so there are any number of things I can say that won't scare people off right away.

Recently I was on my way to a speaking engagement. On the airplane I sat next to a man. He asked me, "What do you do?" I said, "You wouldn't believe it."

He said, "No, really, what do you do?"

"Why don't you guess," I invited.

"Give me a clue," he replied.

I said, "Well, let me see, what's a good clue? I know—I

work for one of the largest organizations in the entire world.''

"Ahh, you work for Union Seventy-Six!"

I said, "No."

"Chevron Oil?"

I said, "No."

"Shell Oil!"

"No."

He said, "Oh."

I could see he needed more clues. So I said, "We are, without question, the first people into a foreign and primitive country, always the first ones in."

"Ahh," he said. "You work for Coca-Cola!"

"No, I don't work for Coca-Cola."

He said, "Let me see, big corporation. First ones in. . . ."

I said, "Yes, we're the first ones to translate languages when we go into a country so we can better distribute our services there."

"Oh! You work for the government."

"No, I don't work for the United States. But I'll give you a couple more clues. We have about three billion associates. On our board of governors are several past presidents of the United States, and Ronald Reagan has publicly professed that he is on our board as well."

By this time my friend was stumped. He said, "Okay, I give up. What *do* you do?"

I smiled and said, "I'm a minister."

Well, I had to catch him on his way down so he wouldn't hurt himself, and then I shared with him why I believe the Christian faith includes the finest people in the world.

I really mean that. I hear a lot about hypocrites and phonies in the church, and I still say you won't find finer people than Christians. They're the best—the cream of the crop. They don't go around lording it over everybody else or looking down on them. But when you become a Christian, you become so much better than you would be if you weren't a Christian. For every phony and hypocrite I've seen in the church, I've seen dozens of people whose lives have been completely transformed, turned around, and filled with love, joy, peace, prosperity, wholeness, and health because they have put their faith in Jesus.

This Race Is in the Right Place

When you join Christ's team, you make two wonderful discoveries:

1. God comes to the place where you are with His message of freedom and challenge.
2. You can go anyplace you want with Him.

When I accepted that ticket to the Olympic Games ceremonies, the invitation was certainly in the right place. The Olympics were in Los Angeles, just a few miles away. I didn't have to go to Moscow, Peking, Iran, or Libya to accept the offer.

The Olympics I was invited to were in a free country, where I didn't have to worry about martial law, being followed, or being placed under house arrest for some strange reason.

A few years ago my father visited mainland China with his uncle. They traveled inland from Amoy to Changchun with official guides of the Communist regime. While in Changchun they went to church and then returned to their hotel for lunch.

Encouraged by the apparent presence of religious freedom, my father was about to take a little stroll before eating, but he was stopped at the door. He was told he could not leave the hotel, and he remained there under virtual house arrest for four hours!

My father couldn't believe it. He had been in the Soviet Union three times and this was his third trip to the People's

Republic of China. This was the first time he had been confined to his hotel without his approval.

The People's Republic guide, a lovely young girl, tried to explain: "You don't understand, Dr. Schuller—"

My father interrupted her. "I do understand. I understand what freedom is—you don't. If you came to the United States of America, you could travel freely from state to state. There you don't need papers to go from city to city."[6]

When you accept Christ's invitation, He offers freedom, not restrictions. You know you're in the right place!

Jesus invites you to join His team even if you think you aren't ready, or worthy. But no matter where you are or how you feel, no matter how low or how bad you think you have been, no matter what your problem might be, God reaches out and says, "I love you." He comes to you with the invitation you can't refuse!

And when you accept that invitation, your place in life has unlimited possibilities. Now you can run the race of faith and go as far and as fast as possible.

A group of women who lived on a Louisiana bayou were having coffee together and most of them were complaining because they didn't live in the city in luxurious, comfortable homes. They hated their lives in the backwaters of Louisiana on the bayou.

One of the women, however, was a positive possibility thinker. She got so tired of the complaining, faultfinding, and criticizing that she finally said to the rest, "Look, it's true we live on the bayou. And the bayou flows right into the ocean. We've all got boats. We can go anywhere we want from where we are. It's up to us."

When you accept God's invitation to faith and start running His race, it's like having a house on the bayou. God is like the water in the bayou which flows into the river, which flows into the gulf, which flows into the ocean. There is no end to it. And there is no end to God's power and God's possibilities to do something within you.

When you touch faith with God, it's like living on the bayou. You can go anywhere from where you are.[7]

This Race Has the Right Price

When Carol offered me that ticket to the Olympics opening ceremony, the price was right—it didn't cost me a cent! The offer of salvation through Christ doesn't cost a cent either. You can't buy it; you can only accept it as a gift.

It's not to say the gift has no value. Obviously, Carol could have stood out in front of the Coliseum and "scalped" that spare ticket to the opening ceremonies for a tidy sum. The ticket to eternal life that God offers us cost His beloved Son in whom He was well pleased.[8] "God loved the world so much that he gave his only Son so that anyone who believes in him shall not perish but have eternal life."[9]

It is impossible to completely appreciate how much sending His Son cost the heavenly Father. You can get an inkling by thinking of the times you have walked past a jewelry store and stared into the window at all the beautiful jewels. There are all kinds of price tags. You see a little ring for fourteen dollars or a silver neck chain for twenty dollars. And there's an attractive gold bracelet that is only ten dollars!

Suddenly a truly stunning piece of jewelry catches your eye, but the price tag is turned over. You hope it's not too expensive, and you go in and ask a clerk what it costs. He turns the price tag over and you go into shock!

Fine pieces of jewelry, the kind that become lasting family heirlooms, are always made out of the costliest metals and jewels. They are never cheap.

There are parables in the Bible that compare heaven to treasure and pearls of great price—fine jewelry. Heaven is where we find God's perfect love, and that has a high price tag! Real love is like expensive jewelry—it's never cheap and it always calls for the costliest commitments.[10]

God has kept His commitments, but what about ours? If salvation is free, where's the need for our commitment?

When Carol offered me that free ticket, there was no price on it, but there were conditions I had to meet. I had to show up at the Coliseum gate, meet Carol, get my ticket, hand it to the ticket taker, and go in and sit down in my seat.

When God offers us our "free ticket" to salvation, there are conditions that at first look as if a long string might be attached to the whole deal. The Bible tells us that salvation frees us from sin, and at the same time it makes us "slaves to righteousness."[11]

"Aha!" many people say, "I knew it! All this 'salvation is free' stuff is a trick to get me to join the church and put plenty of money into the offering plate. Well, in that case the price is too high—way too high."

God doesn't want just our money or our name on a church roster. He wants *us*. He wants us to be His slaves, but that doesn't mean a life of suffering and pain. To be God's slave means to be totally committed to Him, to run the race He has laid out for us.

"Who wants to be a slave?" somebody asks. "Who wants to live in religious bondage—you can't do this, you can't do that. No thanks."

Good, I'm glad you feel that way. Because all of Christ's slaves are free—*totally free*. It works like this: In biblical days a slave could be granted his freedom. In many cases the freed slave loved his master so much that he chose to remain his "slave" for life and underwent the boring of a hole in his earlobe to signify his commitment. The slave knew that he would never be more free than when he lived with his master and enjoyed all the blessings that provided.

So, when we offer ourselves to God in total commitment, there appears to be a high price for accepting His invitation. That price requires your total heart, soul, mind, and body. But then God does something miraculous: He

Take the faith and run. Go for the Gold!

gives it all back. He gives us true freedom, and now we can run the race with Him because of love, not fear and guilt.

The Prize Is Perfection

Earlier I mentioned that this invitation to run the race of faith is for two kinds of people: new recruits and veterans.

If you've never made the commitment to join the race, here is your chance to sign up. You will be with the right people, in the right place, at the right price. Once you make your commitment to this race of faith, God steps in and says, "You're forgiven, your sins are scrubbed away. You're clean, pure—you have the guarantee of eternal life.

"You are My slave, but you wear no chains. You are free to leave at any time. I trust that My love for you and your love for Me will keep us together."

And then God goes on to say, "You have the faith, you are on My Olympic team. Here's your life, clean, pure, and new—now take the faith and run. Go for the Gold!"

But what if you're a veteran? What if you made a commitment sometime in the past—maybe at your mother's knee, or at a high school camp. Wherever it was, you have been running the race for quite a while and you've gotten tired. Never mind, this invitation is for you, too. That great cloud of witnesses from Faith's Hall of Fame know how you feel. They're cheering you on. They're pulling for you to lose that excess weight, get back in shape, get your feet disentangled, get up and start running again.

During the 1984 Olympics, the whole world watched in fascination as Zola Budd came up behind the pack in the women's fifteen-hundred-meter run. Zola tried to pick her way through and somehow got tangled up with the favorite to win the Gold: Mary Decker. Down went Mary, out of the race. Zola limped on to finish well back from the leaders.

Accusations came quickly from both sides. Mary bitterly denounced Zola for tripping her. Reruns of the incident were inconclusive, but one thing was certain: An error had been made. Somebody had fallen short of the mark.

That's what sin is—a missing of the mark, a breaking of the rules, a making of a mistake that is costly and painful. Sin is always ready to entangle anyone who wants to run the race of faith. To avoid it, you have to keep your eyes on Jesus, the Author and Perfecter of this race of faith. In an earlier chapter we saw that perfection is not performing flawlessly. Perfection in scriptural terms means that you persevere, you hang in there to become mature and complete, the best you can be.

Mary Lou Won the Gold—and Our Hearts

Do you remember seeing perfection in action in women's gymnastics competition during the 1984 Olympic Games?

Mary Lou Retton, 4'11" of coiled explosive muscle, was poised on the ramp for her last turn in the vault. In order to win she needed a perfect 10.

All America held its breath as Mary Lou pounded down the runway, her face an absolute picture of determination. She hit the springboard and then the vault and rose into the air to what seemed like fifteen feet, her body turning and twisting in perfect precision. Her feet landed and she "stuck it," that is, she didn't move a fraction. It was a perfect 10! Everyone in the crowd knew it. Everyone watching TV knew it. It was a formality for the scorekeeper to put up the numbers, but when the 10 went up, the crowd went crazy.

Throughout the Olympic Games I was absolutely amazed by what the athletes could do. They had dedicated themselves to perfection, and again and again they turned in performances that are burned into our memories.

Yet, as dedicated as these athletes are, they do not score a 10 every time. Even Mary Lou didn't get a 10 on every exercise in her routine. And today Mary Lou is far from the perfection she displayed that night. In 1986 she retired from gymnastics, never again to soar to the perfect heights she reached when she won the Olympic Gold in the vault.

Go down the line through every Olympic athlete who ever lived, every gold medalist, and you will not find one who has performed perfectly throughout his or her career. If sin is missing the mark—and it is—then all have sinned and come short of perfection, of God's glory.

Nevertheless, the prize at the end of our race of faith is perfection. Thousands of Olympic athletes perform, but only a handful win medals. Every runner in the race of faith, however, is guaranteed the top prize when he fastens his eyes on Jesus, the Author and Perfecter of his faith.

We may stumble, we may falter, we can even get stuck in the mud. There will be times when our flesh will be weaker than our faith. Does that mean God will throw us off the team and have nothing to do with us? No, when we go as far as we possibly can, when we hold on until we can't hold on anymore, when we've come to the end and have to say, "We've done all we can, Lord," He doesn't cast us out. He picks up the baton and runs the race for us. In fact, He carries us across the finish line. He is the Author and Perfecter of our faith.

This is the mystery of grace. I never stop striving to serve Christ, but I also know that my striving isn't what will bring me to the end of the race. My faith is what will bring me to the end. I do not have perfect faith. I do not have total hope. I simply don't have all that it takes to make it. I'm a human being, made of flesh and blood. My faith is like the rest of me, imperfect and incomplete. But the good news is that where my faith falls short, Jesus Christ steps in to perfect it and finish it.

Jesus takes up wherever we leave off. When we can't hold on anymore, He holds on for us.

Our tour of Faith's Hall of Fame has ended. But our race of faith has just begun.

Fix your eyes on Jesus. Take the faith and run the race that is set before you.

Commit yourself to living the best life you can, knowing that God's laws are no longer there to judge you but to be a standard for you to shoot for, just as a gymnast reaches for the perfect 10.

Only through Jesus are your sins washed away.

Only through Jesus are you brought to the finish line and presented a winner—perfect at last.

Believe that what you hope for will happen—and it will.

Believe that what you can't see is really there, up ahead, just around the bend.

Believe you have the power to grow beyond yourself.

Through Christ you can and through Christ you will!

SOURCE NOTES

Introduction

1. *See* Philippians 2:12, 13 PHILLIPS.
2. First Thessalonians 5:17 NASB.
3. From "Don't Quit," by Edgar A. Guest.

Chapter 1
Your Attitude Will Make the Difference

1. Hebrews 11:1 NASB.
2. Hebrews 11:4 TLB.
3. *See* Hebrews 11:4; *see also* Genesis 4:1–7.
4. *See* Genesis 4:7–10. Some commentators believe that the phrase "Your brother's blood cries out to me from the ground" suggests the idea of brutal slaughter.
5. *See* Philippians 4:13.
6. Robert H. Schuller, *Self-Esteem: The New Reformation* (Waco: Word Books, 1982), p. 15.

7. *See* Schuller, *Self-Esteem*, p. 15.
8. *See* Schuller, *Self-Esteem*, pp. 16, 17.
9. *See* Schuller, *Self-Esteem*, p. 17.
10. Rene Dubos, *Celebration of Life* (New York: McGraw-Hill Book Company, 1981).
11. *Robert Schuller's Life Changers*, edited by Robert A. Schuller (Old Tappan, N.J.: Fleming H. Revell Company, 1981), pp. 15, 16.
12. *Life Changers*, pp. 18, 19.

Chapter 2
You Can Break the Fear Barrier—Now!

1. *See* Hebrews 11:4; Genesis 4:1–8.
2. *See* Hebrews 11:5; Genesis 5:21–24; Jude 14, 15.
3. *See* Hebrews 11:5.
4. *See* Genesis 5:21–24.
5. *See* Hebrews 11:6.
6. *See* Hebrews 3:4.
7. Psalms 19:1 NIV.
8. *See* Acts 17:28.
9. *See* Hebrews 11:6 PHILLIPS.
10. Hebrews 11:6 NIV.
11. Jeremiah 29:11 NIV.
12. *See* Matthew 7:7.
13. Hebrews 11:6 NIV.
14. *See* Ephesians 4:17–19.
15. *See* Second Corinthians 5:17; Galatians 5:22–25.

Chapter 3
Commit Yourself to Excellence

1. William James, source unknown.
2. *See* Hebrews 11:7.
3. Thomas J. Peters and Robert H. Waterman, Jr., *In Search of Excellence* (New York: Harper & Row Publishers, Inc., 1982).
4. Ted W. Engstrom, *The Pursuit of Excellence* (Grand Rapids: Zondervan Publishing House, 1982), p. 45.

5. Dr. Denis Waitley, *The Double Win* (Old Tappan, N.J.: Fleming H. Revell Company, 1985), p. 32.
6. Colossians 3:17 NIV.
7. *See* Hebrews 11:5.
8. *See* Genesis 6:9.
9. *See* Genesis 6:22.
10. *See* Harold Lindsell's study note on Genesis 6:14 in *The Living Study Bible* (Wheaton: Tyndale House Publishers, Inc., 1980). Lindsell writes on p. 11: "The ark is a type of Christ who is the place of refuge for sinners who wish to be saved from the wrath to come" (*see* First Peter 3:20, 21).
11. Quoted in Robert H. Schuller, *Self-Esteem: The New Reformation* (Waco: Word Books, 1982), p. 106.
12. Philippians 4:8, 9 NIV.
13. Quoted by Ted Engstrom in *The Pursuit of Excellence* (Grand Rapids: Zondervan Publishing House, 1982), p. 69.
14. Engstrom, *Pursuit,* p. 70.
15. *See* Ken Taylor's *Living Bible* paraphrase of Genesis 6:14–16.
16. *See* Philippians 1:6.
17. For the complete account of the beginnings of Robert H. Schuller's ministry in Garden Grove, California, *see* Robert H. Schuller, *Move Ahead With Possibility Thinking* (New York: Doubleday and Company, Inc., 1967), chapter 2.
18. John W. Gardner, *Excellence* (New York: W. W. Norton & Company, 1984) p. 76.

Chapter 4
Dare to Live by Faith

1. *See* Romans 4:23; Genesis 15:6.
2. *See* Genesis 12:1–3.
3. *See* Hebrews 11:8 NIV.
4. Genesis 12:2, 3 NIV.
5. *See* Genesis 12:4, 5.
6. *See* Genesis 22:2.

7. *See* Genesis 22:1–3.
8. *See* Hebrews 11:19.
9. *See* Genesis 22:4–18.
10. *See* John 14:12–14 NIV.
11. *See* Genesis 12:10–20.
12. *See* Genesis 13:16.
13. Quoted by Denis Waitley in *Seeds of Greatness* (Old Tappan, N.J.: Fleming H. Revell Company, 1983), pp. 169, 170.
14. Waitley, *Seeds*, p. 170.
15. *See* Ephesians 2:8, 9; Colossians 1:13.
16. *See* Ephesians 2:10.
17. First John 3:2 NIV.
18. *See* Psalms 103:15–17; Isaiah 40:6–8.
19. *See* Jeremiah 29:11.

Chapter 5
Learn the Secret of Success

1. *See* Hebrews 11:22.
2. *See* Hebrews 11:23. For an account of Moses' early life, see Exodus 2:1–10.
3. First Kings 3:9 NIV.
4. First Kings 3:12 NIV.
5. *See* Exodus 2:11–14.
6. Proverbs 4:7 NIV.
7. *See* Proverbs 3:14, 8:11.
8. Quoted in *The Pursuit of Excellence* by Ted W. Engstrom (Grand Rapids: Zondervan Publishing House, 1982), pp. 35, 36.
9. This paraphrase of Dorothy Law Nolte's well-known poem was done by Denis Waitley in *The Double Win* (Old Tappan, N.J.: Fleming H. Revell Company, 1985), p. 176.

Chapter 6
Forecast Your Way to Fulfillment

1. *See* Exodus chapters 3 and 4.

2. For the story of how Moses led the Israelites out of Egypt, *see* Exodus, chapters 5 to 14. The account of how Moses led his people through the wilderness is found in the rest of the Book of Exodus, the Book of Leviticus, the Book of Numbers, and the Book of Deuteronomy.
3. *See* Genesis 12:1.
4. *See* Philippians 4:13.
5. *See* Robert A. Schuller, *Getting Through the Going-Through Stage* (Nashville: Thomas Nelson Publishers, 1986), p. 31.
6. Denis Waitley, *The Double Win* (Old Tappan, N.J.: Fleming H. Revell Company, 1985), p. 124.
7. Ari Kiev, *A Strategy for Daily Living* (New York: Free Press, 1973), p. 3.
8. Quoted in *The Pursuit of Excellence* by Ted W. Engstrom (Grand Rapids: Zondervan Publishing House, 1982), p. 85.
9. *See* First Kings 18:16–19:3.
10. *See* Job 3:25.
11. *See* Denis Waitley, *Seeds of Greatness* (Old Tappan, N.J.: Fleming H. Revell Company, 1983), pp. 197, 198.
12. Ray A. Kroc, *Grinding It Out* (New York: Berkley Books, 1978), p. 201.

Chapter 7
Hope Against Hope When It's Hopeless!

1. *See*, for example, *Robert H. Schuller Tells You How to Be an Extraordinary Person in an Ordinary World*, edited by Robert A. Schuller (Old Tappan, N.J.: Fleming H. Revell Company, 1985), p. 147.
2. Hebrews 11:1 NIV.
3. Hebrews 11:1 NASB.
4. *See* Romans 4.
5. *See* Exodus 19, 20.
6. *See* Genesis 17:17.
7. *See* Genesis 21.

8. *See* Genesis 15:1–6.
9. *See* Matthew 6:25–34, 10:20–31.
10. First Corinthians 10:13 PHILLIPS.
11. Job 13:15 NASB.
12. *See* Joni Eareckson and Joe Musser, *Joni* (Grand Rapids: Zondervan Publishing House, 1976), and Joni Eareckson and Steve Estes, *A Step Further* (Grand Rapids: Zondervan Publishing House, 1978).
13. Joni Eareckson Tada, *Choices. . . Changes* (Grand Rapids: Zondervan Publishing House, 1986).
14. Robert A. Schuller, *Getting Through the Going-Through Stage* (Nashville: Thomas Nelson Publishers, 1986).
15. Quoted in *Tough Times Never Last, But Tough People Do!* by Robert H. Schuller (Nashville: Thomas Nelson Publishers, 1983), p. 236.

Chapter 8
Give and Get Back Even More

1. *Robert Schuller's Life Changers*, edited by Robert A. Schuller (Old Tappan, NJ.: Fleming H. Revell Company, 1981), pp. 120–122.
2. *See* Joshua 2.
3. M. Scott Peck, *The Road Less Traveled* (New York: Simon and Schuster, a Touchstone Book, 1978), p. 160.
4. *See* Hebrews 11:1.
5. *Robert H. Schuller Tells You How to Be an Extraordinary Person in an Ordinary World*, edited by Robert A. Schuller (Old Tappan, N.J.: Fleming H. Revell Company, 1985), pp. 113, 114.
6. Second Corinthians 9:7.
7. *See* Luke 6:38.
8. From *The Positive Family* by Arvella Schuller (New York: Doubleday and Company, 1982).
9. *See* Robert H. Schuller, *Tough Times Never Last, But Tough People Do!* (Nashville: Thomas Nelson Publishers, 1983), p. 106.

Chapter 9
Take the Faith and Run the Race!

1. *See* Hebrews 11:32.
2. *See* Hebrews 11:33.
3. *See* Hebrews 11:34–38.
4. *See* Hebrews 11:39, 40.
5. Hebrews 12:1, 2 NIV
6. See *Robert H. Schuller Tells You How to Be an Extraordinary Person in an Ordinary World,* edited by Robert A. Schuller (Old Tappan, N.J.: Fleming H. Revell Company, 1985), p. 95.
7. Schuller, *Extraordinary Person,* p. 52.
8. *See* Matthew 3:17.
9. *See* John 3:16 TLB.
10. Adapted from *Robert Schuller's Life Changers,* edited by Robert A. Schuller (Old Tappan, N.J.: Fleming H. Revell Company, 1981), p. 71.
11. Romans 6:18.

New York Times bestsellers—
Books at their best!